SUSAN W. REDDIN

COMMANDOS ORIGINS

GAME GUIDE

Master Stealth, Combat, and Multi-Character Coordination to Conquer Every Mission

TABLE OF CONTENT

INTRODUCTION

OVERVIEW OF *Commandos: Origins*

Commandos: Origins marks a thrilling return to the beloved *Commandos* series, reimagining the foundations of tactical gameplay in a gripping prequel that sets the stage for the iconic real-time strategy mechanics that made its predecessors so revered. Developed by Claymore Game Studios and published by Kalypso Media, *Commandos: Origins* draws players back into the chaos of World War II, but this time, you'll experience the formation of the elite commando unit from its very inception.

As an avid gamer, stepping into this game feels like revisiting a world that has shaped the tactical genre. However, *Commandos: Origins* is far from being a mere rehash of its predecessors. With its polished mechanics, diverse environments, and fresh storyline, the game introduces new twists while honoring the essence of the *Commandos* franchise. Every mission is meticulously crafted to challenge even the most seasoned players while offering newcomers a chance to immerse themselves in an environment rich with tactical depth and strategic variety.

Unlike many traditional tactical games, *Commandos: Origins* places a strong emphasis on the real-time strategy elements that require careful planning, stealth, and timing. Each mission pushes players to think multiple steps ahead, whether they're quietly infiltrating enemy lines, taking down guards from a distance, or using the environment to create distractions. The beauty of the game lies in its flexibility there's no one-size-fits-all solution to the challenges you face, which means every mission can be approached in a variety of ways depending on your preferred style of play.

One of the most exciting elements of the game is the ability to control a team of diverse characters, each with unique skills. From the Green Beret's brute strength to the Sniper's precision, and the Spy's ability to blend into enemy ranks, *Commandos: Origins* ensures that every character plays a vital role in achieving mission success. This dynamic approach to gameplay allows for strategic depth, requiring players to carefully manage and utilize the strengths of each commando to tackle challenges.

The rich visual design and historical accuracy of the settings provide a deeply immersive experience. Players will traverse landscapes ranging from dense forests and fortified enemy bases to coastal towns under siege, all while interacting with NPCs, gathering intel, and solving complex puzzles. It's a world that demands patience, precision, and a sharp tactical mind.

Commandos: Origins also stands out by introducing cooperative play, allowing friends to team up and take on missions together. This addition provides a fresh layer of excitement to the gameplay, as coordination between players becomes key to completing objectives. Whether you're navigating a hostile environment or trying to outsmart enemy forces, having a partner by your side elevates the strategic experience to new heights.

With the game's impending release in April 2025, the excitement among *Commandos* fans and newcomers alike is palpable. This is not just a game; it's a journey back to the roots of tactical strategy, where every move count, and every decision is critical. Whether you're a long-time fan of the series or a first-time player, *Commandos: Origins* promises to deliver an unforgettable gaming experience that will challenge your mind and push your skills to their limits.

This guide aims to help you navigate the complexities of the game with ease, providing you with expert tips, mission walkthroughs, and strategies that will ensure you're fully equipped to tackle every challenge *Commandos: Origins* has to offer. So, whether you're infiltrating enemy camps or masterminding the perfect ambush, this guide will be your trusted companion on the road to victory.

A BRIEF HISTORY OF THE COMMANDOS SERIES

The *Commandos* series, first released in 1998, is a defining title in the real-time tactics genre, developed by the Spanish company Pyro Studios. Known for its innovative gameplay, challenging mechanics, and intricate level design, *Commandos* set itself apart from the traditional strategy games of its time. The game combined tactical decision-making with real-time action, demanding precision, patience, and careful planning from players. It quickly became a fan favorite and is remembered for its strategic depth and difficulty, laying the groundwork for many tactical games that followed.

The first game in the series, *Commandos: Behind Enemy Lines*, introduced players to a small team of highly specialized soldiers who must infiltrate enemy territory, sabotage operations, and complete dangerous missions in World War II. Each member of the team had distinct skills from the strong

Green Beret to the stealthy Spy requiring players to manage their characters carefully to succeed. This set the tone for the series, as players had to use their wits more than their firepower, planning and executing each mission with precision.

The success of *Commandos: Behind Enemy Lines* led to the development of several sequels and expansions, each further expanding the series' tactical depth. *Commandos 2: Men of Courage* (2001) brought improved 3D graphics and enhanced gameplay, with larger and more complex missions. It introduced additional characters and greater flexibility in how missions could be approached. This sequel became one of the most praised entries in the series, and its success cemented *Commandos* as a franchise to watch.

Commandos 3: Destination Berlin (2003) followed, refining the gameplay further with a more streamlined experience. While it wasn't as beloved as its predecessors, *Commandos 3* still offered an engaging tactical experience, with new mission types and updated graphics. The series continued to garner a dedicated fanbase, though by this point, it had begun to show its age in comparison to the growing landscape of more modern tactical games.

Despite the series' popularity, it went into a long hiatus, with no new releases in the following years. Fans of *Commandos* had to make do with re-releases of the older titles, as well as rumors of a potential new installment. This hiatus lasted until *Commandos: Origins* was officially announced, re-igniting the flames of nostalgia and excitement among loyal fans.

Commandos: Origins brings the franchise back to its roots, offering a fresh take on the tactical gameplay that made the original titles so special. This prequel not only explores the formation of the elite commando unit but also introduces modern gameplay enhancements, cooperative play, and improved graphics. The latest game stays true to the series' tactical roots while adapting to new gaming trends and technologies. With *Commandos: Origins*, players get to relive the thrill of outwitting enemy forces using strategy, stealth, and teamwork, all while diving deeper into the backstory of the iconic characters they've come to love over the years.

Through the evolution of its gameplay and story, the *Commandos* series has maintained a unique place in the gaming world, and *Commandos: Origins* promises to breathe new life into this legendary franchise. Whether you're a veteran of the series or a newcomer to the world of tactical gameplay, *Commandos: Origins* offers a captivating experience that honors the legacy of its predecessors while introducing exciting new features for modern audiences.

WHAT'S NEW IN *Commandos: Origins*?

Commandos: Origins introduces several notable enhancements and features that modernize the classic tactical gameplay while honoring its legacy. Developed by Claymore Game Studios and set for release on April 9, 2025, the game offers both returning fans and newcomers a refreshed experience.

Modernized Loot System

Responding to community feedback, the developers have implemented a modernized loot system that replaces the traditional inventory approach. Enemies now drop items such as ammunition and first aid kits upon defeat. Additionally, players can find collectibles and enemy uniforms in various locations. These items are immediately accessible through each commando's unique abilities, streamlining gameplay and enhancing strategic options.

Non-Lethal Combat Options

To add depth to tactical choices, *Commandos: Origins* introduces non-lethal combat methods. Players can temporarily incapacitate enemies, allowing for stealthier approaches and diverse mission strategies. This feature encourages thoughtful engagement with the game's challenges.

Enhanced AI Behavior

The game features improved artificial intelligence, ensuring that enemy reactions are realistic and dynamic. This enhancement requires players to adapt their strategies, as AI behavior is more responsive and unpredictable, contributing to a more immersive experience.

Expanded Map Design

Addressing feedback about previous demos, the developers have designed larger, more open maps in the full game. These expansive environments offer multiple approaches to mission objectives, enhancing replayability and strategic planning.

Command Mode Feature

A new "Command Mode" allows players to pause the game and issue orders to individual commandos. This feature facilitates precise coordination, enabling complex strategies to be executed effectively. Once orders are set, actions can be carried out simultaneously, streamlining gameplay.

Cooperative Multiplayer

Commandos: Origins supports cooperative multiplayer, both online and via local split-screen. This addition allows friends to team up, combining their tactical skills to overcome challenges, fostering collaboration and enhancing the game's strategic elements.

Enhanced User Interface and Controls

Recognizing the need for modern usability, the game features an updated user interface with customizable controls. Players can adjust keybindings and choose from various control schemes, tailoring the experience to their preferences.

These developments aim to provide a rich, engaging experience that respects the series' origins while embracing modern gaming advancements.

THE GOAL OF THIS GUIDE

The primary goal of this guide is to provide you with a comprehensive and practical resource to master *Commandos: Origins*, no matter your skill level. Whether you're a seasoned *Commandos* veteran or a newcomer to the series, this guide is designed to enhance your gameplay experience by offering expert strategies, insightful tips, and in-depth walkthroughs that will help you navigate every challenge the game throws your way.

This guide aims to empower you with the knowledge to:

1. Master the Mechanics

From understanding the core gameplay features to mastering the unique abilities of each commando, this guide will walk you through the essential mechanics of the game. We'll cover how to effectively control your team, utilize the environment, and optimize your tactical approaches to achieve mission success.

2. Understand the Characters

Each commando in *Commandos: Origins* has specialized skills that are key to your success. This guide will break down the strengths and weaknesses of each character, so you can deploy them strategically based on the objectives of the mission. Whether it's the Sniper's long-range precision or the Spy's stealth abilities, you'll learn how to make the most of each role.

3. Navigate Through Every Mission

The heart of *Commandos: Origins* lies in its missions, and this guide offers detailed walkthroughs of each mission, ensuring you understand the objectives, challenges, and the best approaches to overcoming them. We'll provide step-by-step instructions, highlight key tactics, and even reveal some hidden secrets and collectibles you might miss if you're not careful.

4. Tackle Advanced Strategies

As you progress, the difficulty of the game ramps up, requiring more complex strategies. This guide goes beyond the basics to teach you advanced tactics, including how to manage multiple characters in difficult scenarios, coordinate your team for complex operations, and use the environment to your advantage. We'll also explore how to tackle higher difficulty levels and unlock hidden achievements.

5. Enhance Replayability

With multiple ways to approach each mission and countless strategies to explore, *Commandos: Origins* offers a high level of replayability. This guide will provide you with the tools to experiment with different tactics, encouraging you to revisit missions and try new approaches, ensuring that no two playthroughs are ever the same.

6. Provide Helpful Resources

Whether you need help troubleshooting technical issues or you want to learn about the community resources available for *Commandos: Origins*, this guide will provide links to essential forums, mods, and behind-the-scenes content to help you dive deeper into the game.

By the end of this guide, you'll be fully equipped with everything you need to tackle *Commandos: Origins* like a true expert, maximizing your enjoyment of the game while achieving top-tier performance. Our goal is to ensure that you feel confident, informed, and ready to conquer every mission the game offers, from the first skirmish to the final assault.

CHAPTER 1: GETTING STARTED

1.1 INSTALLING AND LAUNCHING THE GAME

Commandos: Origins is an exciting tactical strategy game that demands precision and critical thinking right from the moment you start. Before you can embark on your mission as an elite commando, it's essential to get the game up and running smoothly on your system. In this section, we'll guide you through the installation process and walk you through launching the game to ensure a smooth start.

System Requirements

To ensure optimal performance, it's important to verify that your system meets or exceeds the minimum requirements. Here are the details for both the **minimum** and **recommended** system configurations:

Component	Minimum Requirements	Recommended Requirements
Operating System	Windows 10 (64-bit)	Windows 10 or 11 (64-bit)
Processor	Intel Core i5-7600 / AMD Ryzen 5 1600	Intel Core i7-9700 / AMD Ryzen 7 3700X
Memory	8 GB RAM	16 GB RAM
Graphics	NVIDIA GeForce GTX 960 / AMD Radeon R9 380	NVIDIA GeForce RTX 2070 / AMD Radeon RX 5700 XT
DirectX	Version 11	Version 12
Storage	40 GB available space	40 GB available space
Sound	DirectX compatible sound card	DirectX compatible sound card

Downloading the Game

Once you've confirmed that your system meets the requirements, the next step is downloading *Commandos: Origins*. The game is available through several digital storefronts, including Steam, Epic Games Store, and Xbox Game Pass.

1. **Steam**
   - Open the Steam client on your PC.
   - Use the search bar to find *Commandos: Origins*.
   - Click "Add to Cart" and proceed to checkout.
   - Once purchased, the game will automatically start downloading.
2. **Epic Games Store**
   - Open the Epic Games Launcher.
   - Search for *Commandos: Origins*.
   - After purchasing, the download will begin automatically.
3. **Xbox Game Pass**
   - If you have an Xbox Game Pass subscription, search for *Commandos: Origins* in the Game Pass library.
   - Click "Install" to begin downloading the game directly to your system.

Installing the Game

After downloading the game, follow the simple installation steps:

1. **Steam Installation**
   - Once the download is complete, click "Install" in your Steam library.
   - Choose the destination folder for the game installation and confirm.
   - Steam will then automatically install the game for you.
2. **Epic Games Store Installation**
   - After the download finishes, the game will automatically begin installing.
   - If prompted, select the installation directory and proceed.
3. **Xbox Game Pass Installation**
   - The game will begin installing automatically once you click "Install" from the Game Pass library.

o   You can choose to install it on the default drive or select a custom location for the installation.

Launching the Game

Once the game is successfully installed, it's time to launch and dive into the action. Follow these steps to get started:

1. **Steam**
   - o   Open the Steam client.
   - o   Navigate to your Library and click on *Commandos: Origins*.
   - o   Click the "Play" button to launch the game.
2. **Epic Games Store**
   - o   Open the Epic Games Launcher.
   - o   Go to your Library and select *Commandos: Origins*.
   - o   Press "Launch" to start the game.
3. **Xbox Game Pass**
   - o   Open the Xbox app or Game Pass client.
   - o   Find *Commandos: Origins* in your library.
   - o   Click "Play" to start the game.

First-Time Setup

When you launch *Commandos: Origins* for the first time, you may need to configure a few settings before starting your first mission:

1. **Graphics Settings**
   - o   You'll be prompted to select your preferred resolution and graphics quality settings. Choose the settings that best match your system's capabilities.
   - o   You can adjust these later in the game's options menu, but it's recommended to start with the default settings if you're unsure.
2. **Audio Settings**
   - o   Ensure that your sound output (headphones, speakers, etc.) is correctly set up. You can also adjust the game's audio levels, including music, effects, and dialogue.
3. **Control Configuration**
   - o   You can customize the key bindings to suit your personal preferences. The game will allow you to configure controls

for both keyboard and mouse, as well as gamepads if you prefer using one.

4. **Saving and Loading**
    o   *Commandos: Origins* uses an auto-save system that ensures you never lose significant progress. However, you can also manually save at any time, especially during key moments in missions.

Common Installation Issues

If you encounter any issues during installation or launch, here are a few troubleshooting tips:

1. **Corrupted Installation Files**
    o   Verify the integrity of the game files on Steam or Epic Games Store. Both platforms offer a repair feature that will re-download any corrupted files.
2. **Low Storage Space**
    o   Ensure you have enough disk space on your drive for both the game and any future updates or expansions. If space is limited, consider uninstalling unused programs or moving files to an external storage device.
3. **Driver Updates**
    o   Ensure your graphics card drivers are up to date. You can check for updates through NVIDIA GeForce Experience or AMD Radeon Software.
4. **DirectX or Visual C++ Redistributables**
    o   If the game doesn't launch, check that you have the latest version of DirectX installed. You can download it from the official Microsoft website. Similarly, ensure your Visual C++ Redistributables are updated.

1.2 UNDERSTANDING THE INTERFACE AND CONTROLS

To succeed in *Commandos: Origins*, you'll need to become familiar with the game's interface and controls, as these are crucial to executing tactical maneuvers and strategizing your next move. The game's interface is designed to be intuitive for players of all experience levels, with a focus on providing you with the necessary information without overwhelming you with too much on-screen clutter.

The Main Interface

When you first load into the game, you'll be greeted with a clean, strategic interface that allows you to easily manage your commandos and assess the battlefield. Here's an overview of the main elements you'll encounter:

1. **Top Bar**
   - **Mission Objectives**: Displays a brief summary of the active mission objectives. This section allows you to stay focused on your goals as you progress through the game. You can quickly check what's left to accomplish without having to pause the game.
   - **Timer (if applicable)**: For missions with a time constraint, a timer will appear here. It counts down until you must complete the objectives, adding an additional layer of pressure and excitement to your strategy.
   - **Current Progress/Intel**: Displays important mission information, such as acquired intel, number of enemies defeated, or critical objectives achieved. This section also offers hints if you're stuck, providing subtle direction without being overly prescriptive.
2. **Center Panel**
   - **Game View**: This is where most of the action takes place. The game's top-down camera view gives you a detailed perspective of the environment, your commandos, and enemy forces. You can zoom in and out to better analyze the terrain or focus on smaller areas. The camera can be rotated for optimal angles, giving you a full 360-degree view of the battlefield.
   - **Mini-Map**: Situated in the corner of the screen, the mini-map gives you an overview of the current environment. It helps you spot key locations, enemy units, and points of interest, all while allowing you to navigate faster.
   - **Character Stats**: Below the main game view, you'll find each commando's stats and health bar. As you control the commandos, these indicators update in real-time, providing you with immediate feedback on their status. Knowing when a commando is injured, tired, or low on resources is crucial for successful missions.

3. **Bottom Bar**
   o **Action Buttons**: This area is where you'll issue commands to your commandos. You can click on your commando to bring up a list of available actions (such as move, attack, use special skills, etc.), or you can use hotkeys for quicker access.
   o **Inventory**: Each commando has a personal inventory for weapons, tools, and items they collect. You can open this panel to manage the equipment your character is carrying and quickly assign items to be used during the mission.
   o **Quick Save/Load**: This is where you can save or load your game at any moment. Quick saves allow you to preserve your progress, while quick load lets you restart from the last point to refine your strategy.

Control Scheme

Understanding the control layout will help you issue commands swiftly and without hesitation, a vital skill in tactical games where time and precision matter.

Mouse Controls

- **Left-Click**: Select a commando, issue movement commands, or interact with objects in the environment. Left-clicking also allows you to engage with enemies (for combat or sabotage).
- **Right-Click**: Use the right mouse button to access additional options for the selected commando, like issuing special abilities or opening the inventory. It's also used to cancel orders or deselect units.
- **Scroll Wheel**: Zoom in or out of the game world, adjusting the camera view to either focus on small details or get a broader perspective of the battlefield.

Keyboard Controls

- **W, A, S, D**: Move the camera across the battlefield. This allows you to quickly explore the environment and see areas beyond your direct line of sight.

- **Spacebar**: Pause the game. This is especially useful in tactical games, allowing you to plan your next steps carefully before issuing more orders.
- **1-6 Keys**: These numbers correspond to the different commandos in your squad. Pressing the number of a commando will select them, enabling you to quickly jump between units during combat or exploration.
- **Q**: Quick save your progress. It's a good practice to save regularly during difficult or dangerous missions.
- **E**: Quick load the most recent saved game. This allows you to retry a mission from a previous checkpoint if things go wrong.

Special Commands

- **Ctrl + 1-6**: Assign a commando to a hotkey for easy access later. This is especially useful if you need to quickly switch between commandos during fast-paced situations.
- **Shift**: Hold the shift key to queue multiple actions for a selected commando. For example, you can command your commando to move to one location and then immediately engage in combat when they arrive.
- **Tab**: Toggle between the available objectives or map modes, allowing you to track your mission progress and identify key areas on the map.

Managing Multiple Commandos

In *Commandos: Origins*, the real challenge lies in managing multiple characters at once. With your team of elite commandos, each with unique abilities, you need to effectively coordinate their actions to succeed in missions. Here are some tips for managing multiple units:

1. **Using Grouping Commands**:
   - Press **Ctrl + 1-6** to group specific commandos together, allowing you to issue commands to the group as a whole. This is especially useful for combined attacks or strategic movements.
   - You can also use the **Shift key** to queue actions across multiple commandos, ensuring that each character performs their tasks in sync.
2. **Assigning Roles**:

- o Each commando has their strengths. Use this to your advantage by assigning roles based on mission requirements. For example, the Spy should be used for stealth and infiltration, while the Green Beret can be tasked with heavy combat.

3. **Camera Control**:
   - o Use the camera controls to keep track of all your commandos, especially in larger environments. The mini-map will also help you monitor their positions and movements at all times, ensuring they stay in sync.

User Interface Customization

You can adjust several aspects of the interface to suit your preferences:

1. **Control Scheme Adjustments**:
   - o You can customize the keybindings through the options menu to ensure you're comfortable with your control setup. This allows for flexibility if you have a personal preference or if you're using a gamepad.
2. **UI Scaling**:
   - o The game provides options to scale the UI elements. If you prefer larger icons or a more compact display, you can modify these settings in the graphics options.
3. **Audio/Visual Settings**:
   - o In the options menu, you can adjust sound levels for music, sound effects, and dialogue. You can also toggle subtitles for mission briefings or character conversations.

1.3 SETTING UP YOUR PREFERENCES

Setting up your preferences in *Commandos: Origins* is an essential step in tailoring the game to your needs, ensuring that you have the most comfortable and efficient gaming experience possible. This section will guide you through the various settings available and show you how to optimize them for your playstyle, whether you prefer a smooth, easy experience or are looking for a more challenging, hardcore tactical adventure.

Adjusting Graphics Settings

To ensure smooth gameplay and enhance your visual experience, it's important to configure your graphics settings based on your system's capabilities. Here's how you can optimize the graphics settings:

1. **Resolution**:
   - Go to the **Display** settings to choose your screen resolution. The higher the resolution, the crisper and more detailed the visuals will be, but it requires more processing power. If you're running on higher-end hardware, 1080p or 1440p is recommended. For mid-range systems, 720p or 1080p works well.
   - **Tip**: If you experience performance issues, try lowering the resolution or enabling **dynamic resolution scaling** to maintain a steady framerate.
2. **Texture Quality**:
   - *Commandos: Origins* offers different texture quality levels: **Low**, **Medium**, **High**, and **Ultra**. Higher quality textures improve visual fidelity, especially for detailed environments, but can impact performance.
   - **Tip**: If your system struggles with performance, lowering the texture quality will improve frame rates without sacrificing too much visual appeal.
3. **Anti-Aliasing**:
   - Anti-aliasing smooths out jagged edges in the game's graphics. It's essential for ensuring sharp, clear visuals, but it can be demanding on your system.
   - **Tip**: For high-end systems, enable **TAA (Temporal Anti-Aliasing)** or **FXAA (Fast Approximate Anti-Aliasing)** for smoother edges without losing performance.
4. **V-Sync and Frame Rate**:
   - **V-Sync** prevents screen tearing, ensuring a smoother visual experience. However, it can introduce input lag, especially on lower framerate setups.
   - **Frame Rate Limit**: You can set a frame rate cap (60 FPS is typically good for most systems). If you're using a monitor with a high refresh rate, you may opt for higher frame rates, but this depends on your hardware's capabilities.
   - **Tip**: If you have a high refresh rate monitor (120Hz or above), you may want to disable V-Sync for smoother performance.
5. **Post-Processing Effects**:

- These include settings like **Motion Blur**, **Depth of Field**, and **Bloom**. While these effects can make the game more visually appealing, they can also decrease performance.
- **Tip**: If you prefer a more visually realistic experience, turn on Post-Processing effects. If performance is a concern, disabling them can help maintain a steady frame rate.

Adjusting Audio Settings

The audio in *Commandos: Origins* plays a crucial role in the immersive experience. Ensuring your audio preferences are set correctly can significantly enhance gameplay, especially when it comes to in-game sound cues such as enemy movements or environmental sounds.

1. **Master Volume**:
   - Adjust the overall game volume to your preference. Set it to a level where you can clearly hear both the background music and the sound effects, but without overpowering the game's dialogue and voice lines.
   - **Tip**: If you use headphones, you may want to lower the overall volume to protect your ears during extended sessions.
2. **Sound Effects and Music**:
   - The **Sound Effects** volume controls the in-game sounds, such as footsteps, gunfire, and explosions. The **Music** volume controls the background soundtrack.
   - **Tip**: For a more immersive experience, you may want the sound effects to be louder than the music, allowing you to hear all environmental cues.
3. **Dialogue and Voice Lines**:
   - This slider adjusts the volume of the game's voice acting, which plays a crucial role in understanding the context of the missions and character interactions.
   - **Tip**: If you're a fan of the narrative and want to catch every line of dialogue, set this slider to a higher level.
4. **Speech Language**:
   - You can change the language of the voiceovers from English to various other languages, depending on your preference.
   - **Tip**: If you're playing the game in a language you're not familiar with, consider enabling subtitles for a smoother experience.

Control Preferences

Commandos: Origins provides flexibility in how you interact with the game, allowing you to choose between different control schemes. Whether you prefer a keyboard and mouse setup or a gamepad, this section will guide you in customizing your controls.

1. **Key Mapping**:
   o You can remap the controls to suit your personal preferences. The default controls are functional, but if you find certain key bindings uncomfortable or unintuitive, you can easily change them here.
   o **Tip**: Many players prefer reassigning the **1-6** keys (for selecting commandos) to something more convenient, such as numbers on the keypad for quicker access.
2. **Mouse Sensitivity**:
   o Adjusting the **Mouse Sensitivity** lets you fine-tune the responsiveness of your mouse. This is especially important for aiming or controlling precise movements in the game.
   o **Tip**: If you have a high-DPI mouse, you might want to lower the sensitivity to ensure smoother and more precise movements in-game.
3. **Gamepad Support**:
   o If you prefer using a controller, *Commandos: Origins* supports gamepads, including Xbox and PlayStation controllers.
   o **Tip**: For a more console-like experience, connect your controller before launching the game to have it automatically detected.
4. **Camera Controls**:
   o The camera is essential for managing your units effectively in tactical games. Adjust the sensitivity of the camera movement and rotation to fit your playstyle.
   o **Tip**: If you prefer fast, agile camera movements, increase the sensitivity slightly. If you like more controlled, slower movements, decrease it for precision.

Gameplay Settings

In addition to visual and control preferences, there are gameplay-specific settings that influence how the game functions during your missions.

1. **Difficulty Level**:
   - o Choose between different difficulty levels: **Easy, Normal**, or **Hard**. This choice affects enemy AI intelligence, mission constraints, and the level of strategic thinking required to succeed.
   - o **Tip**: If you're new to the *Commandos* series or prefer a more relaxed experience, start with **Easy** difficulty. For veteran players, **Hard** offers a greater challenge.
2. **HUD Display Options**:
   - o Customize the display of on-screen information (such as health bars, mission objectives, and the mini-map). You can choose to turn off certain HUD elements if you prefer a cleaner, more immersive experience.
   - o **Tip**: Turning off unnecessary elements can help focus your attention on the strategy rather than the interface.
3. **Auto-Save**:
   - o The game features an auto-save function, but you can adjust how frequently the game auto-saves during your missions. Setting a lower frequency may increase tension, as you'll need to manually save your progress more often.
   - o **Tip**: For newcomers, it's recommended to keep auto-save enabled at frequent intervals to avoid losing progress.

Finalizing Your Preferences

Once you've adjusted all the settings to your liking, it's time to save your preferences. Simply click on the **Apply** button to confirm your changes. You can always revisit this menu if you feel the need to tweak anything as you play, ensuring your settings evolve along with your experience in *Commandos: Origins*.

1.4 TIPS FOR NEW PLAYERS

Commandos: Origins is a game that rewards careful planning, patience, and tactical decision-making. As a newcomer, you might feel overwhelmed by the complexity of managing multiple characters and navigating the battlefield. However, with the right mindset and a few helpful tips, you'll be able to dive into the game with confidence and start mastering its mechanics. Here are some tips to help you get started and set you on the path to success:

1. Take Your Time to Learn the Controls

One of the biggest challenges for new players is getting comfortable with the controls and understanding how to issue commands efficiently. Spend a few minutes in the training missions or practice areas to familiarize yourself with the basic controls:

- **Move and Select Characters**: Use the mouse and keyboard to select commandos, issue movement orders, and zoom in or out on the environment. The **1-6** keys are your shortcut to quickly switching between characters.
- **Pause and Plan**: Don't be afraid to pause the game using the **Spacebar** to plan your next moves. This is especially important in tactical games like *Commandos: Origins*, where thinking ahead is key.

2. Master Stealth and Patience

While combat is a significant aspect of the game, *Commandos: Origins* places a heavy emphasis on stealth. You'll often be faced with situations where avoiding detection is the best course of action. Here's how to master stealth:

- **Use the Environment**: Hide behind objects like trees, rocks, or walls to remain out of sight from enemy patrols. Pay attention to guard patrol routes and plan your movements accordingly.
- **Quiet and Cautious Movements**: Move slowly by holding down the **Shift** key, which ensures your character makes less noise and is harder to detect.
- **Take Out Guards Quietly**: When you need to eliminate enemies, opt for non-lethal takedowns when possible to avoid drawing attention. Use a commando like the Spy for stealthy infiltrations.

3. Use Your Commandos' Unique Skills

Each commando in *Commandos: Origins* has distinct abilities, and understanding how to use them effectively will make or break your success in missions:

- **The Green Beret**: He is great for hand-to-hand combat and has the ability to carry heavy items. Use him for direct assaults or when you need to clear a path for your team.

- **The Sniper**: His long-range precision is invaluable. Position him at higher ground or in a concealed spot to pick off enemies from a distance without alerting others.
- **The Sapper**: Use him to plant explosives and destroy obstacles. He can also disable enemy vehicles or structures that might otherwise be difficult to access.
- **The Spy**: The Spy excels in blending in with the enemy. Use him to gather intel, sneak past guards, or sabotage equipment undetected.
- **The Marine**: With his heavy weaponry, he's perfect for assaulting enemy strongholds or providing cover fire while your other commandos complete objectives.

Each character is vital for different situations, so switch between them strategically during missions. Learn when to use brute force and when to rely on stealth and subterfuge.

4. Plan Ahead Before You Act

Commandos: Origins is a game that rewards thoughtful preparation over hasty action. Always pause before making a move and assess the situation:

- **Observe Enemy Patterns**: Pay attention to enemy patrols, guard placement, and the layout of the area. You can use the **mini-map** to spot potential hazards and identify objectives.
- **Use the Environment to Your Advantage**: Find areas where you can hide or create distractions. For example, you can use a thrown rock to lure enemies away from their posts, making it easier to sneak past them.
- **Quick Save**: It's always a good idea to make frequent use of the quick save function (**Ctrl + S**) in case things go wrong. If you make a mistake, you can quickly load your previous save and adjust your approach.

5. Learn from Your Mistakes

Mistakes are inevitable, but in *Commandos: Origins*, they're a great way to learn. If you fail a mission or get spotted, take a moment to analyze what went wrong and try a different strategy. Maybe a different commando would have been more effective in that situation, or perhaps you moved too quickly and missed an opportunity for stealth.

- **Trial and Error**: Don't be afraid to experiment with different strategies. The game's high replayability means you can try multiple approaches until you find the one that works best for you.

6. Use the Pause Feature to Plan

The **Pause** button (Spacebar) is your best friend in *Commandos: Origins*. Tactical games like this require thoughtful planning, and pausing the game lets you issue commands for all your units at once. This can be invaluable when you need to:

- **Synchronize Attacks**: Set up simultaneous actions for multiple commandos to execute at the same time.
- **Avoid Detection**: Pause the game, observe enemy patrols, and then issue your commands to avoid getting spotted.
- **Set Up Traps and Ambushes**: Pause and plan out your next move in detail, setting traps or positioning your units for the best tactical advantage.

7. Keep Track of Your Resources

In addition to your commandos, you also need to manage your resources. These include items like weapons, ammo, health packs, and explosives. Be mindful of your inventory:

- **Only Carry What You Need**: Each commando has limited space for items, so carry only what's necessary for the mission. Excess weight can slow down your movement and reduce your stealth effectiveness.
- **Search for Items**: Often, you'll need to scavenge the environment for additional items. This can include weapons dropped by enemies, hidden caches, or tools needed to complete objectives.

8. Play Missions in Any Order

While the game has a linear storyline, *Commandos: Origins* offers a degree of flexibility in how you approach missions. If you're struggling with one, don't hesitate to move on to another. This allows you to build up your experience and tackle more difficult objectives when you're ready.

9. Keep Your Commandos Alive

It's easy to get too attached to your units, but in *Commandos: Origins*, keeping all your commandos alive is a priority. While you can sacrifice one commando for tactical reasons, losing too many can make subsequent parts of the mission much more difficult.

- **Healing Items**: Make use of health packs and medical kits when your commandos are injured, and remember to give them rest if they've been running for extended periods.

10. Embrace the Challenge

Finally, embrace the challenge that *Commandos: Origins* offers. It's a game designed for players who love deep strategy, and it can take time to get accustomed to the complexity of the missions and the mechanics. Don't be discouraged if it takes several attempts to complete a mission. Every failure is a learning opportunity, and every victory feels that much more rewarding.

CHAPTER 2: GAMEPLAY MECHANICS

2.1 CORE GAMEPLAY FEATURES

In *Commandos: Origins*, mastering the core gameplay mechanics is essential to succeeding in the game's complex tactical scenarios. The game provides a unique combination of stealth, strategy, and real-time decision-making, which requires players to think several steps ahead while carefully coordinating their squad. This chapter will guide you through the fundamental gameplay features, the mechanics of movement and positioning, and how to use stealth effectively in your missions.

Commandos: Origins offers a rich, immersive tactical experience that emphasizes planning, coordination, and patience. Here's a breakdown of the game's core features that you'll need to master in order to succeed:

1. Multi-Character Control

The hallmark of *Commandos* is the ability to control a team of commandos, each with unique skills and abilities. These commandos must work together to overcome the mission's objectives, which range from sabotage to rescue operations. Each commando is designed for a specific role, and knowing when and how to use each character's strengths is key to completing missions successfully.

Commando	Role	Special Abilities
Green Beret	All-rounder, melee combat	Strong in hand-to-hand combat, carries heavy objects, can lift bodies
Sniper	Long-range combat	Excellent precision, can eliminate enemies from a distance
Sapper	Explosives and demolitions	Can plant explosives, disable traps, and sabotage enemy equipment

Spy	Stealth and deception	Blends in with enemies, can unlock doors and sabotage from within
Driver	Vehicle specialist	Can operate vehicles to traverse environments or attack enemies
Marine	Heavy weapons and combat	Strong in firepower, excels at fighting enemies head-on

Each of these characters can be selected, controlled, and deployed to execute specific tasks. Switching between them frequently allows for strategic flexibility, but it also requires good management and coordination.

2. Environmental Interaction

The environment plays a significant role in *Commandos: Origins*. Unlike many tactical games, *Commandos* allows you to interact with the environment in numerous ways:

- **Cover**: You can hide behind walls, trees, barrels, and other objects to avoid detection or to set up ambushes.
- **Objects and Tools**: Your commandos can pick up various objects (such as crates, rocks, and barrels) and use them for both offensive and defensive strategies. You can also pick up enemy weapons or tools for specific missions.
- **Traps and Hazards**: The game's levels are designed with hidden traps, like land mines or electrified fences, that require careful navigation and, in some cases, disabling by the Sapper.

3. Real-Time Strategy with Pause

One of the unique features of *Commandos: Origins* is its real-time strategy mechanics combined with the ability to pause and plan your next move. During the game, you can pause at any time by pressing **Spacebar**. This allows you to issue commands to all your units at once, giving you a chance to plan and react to changing circumstances without the pressure of real-time execution. However, you need to be quick and efficient with your planning, as the clock ticks on when the game is unpaused.

4. Mission Objectives and Progression

In *Commandos: Origins*, missions vary in complexity and objectives. Some will require stealth and sabotage, while others might demand a full-on assault. You'll be tasked with objectives such as:

- **Infiltration**: Sneak past enemy lines without being detected.
- **Sabotage**: Destroy or disable enemy equipment or facilities.
- **Rescue**: Extract prisoners or VIPs from enemy strongholds.
- **Combat**: Engage and defeat enemy forces in tactical firefights.

You'll need to complete the objectives within the given constraints, whether it's under a strict time limit or while avoiding civilian casualties. Completing these tasks often unlocks new challenges and missions, allowing you to progress through the game.

2.2 STEALTH AND TACTICAL MOVEMENT

Stealth is the foundation of *Commandos: Origins*. Many missions can be completed without engaging in direct combat, making stealth a vital skill for success. Here's how you can use stealth and tactical movement to your advantage.

1. Stealth Mechanics

Stealth in *Commandos: Origins* is about carefully maneuvering your commandos through hostile territory without drawing attention. Key elements of stealth include:

- **Visibility**: Your commandos have a visibility range. If enemies see them, they'll raise alarms, triggering combat or alerting other guards to the area. Stay out of sight by moving between cover and using shadows to your advantage.
- **Noise**: When moving or interacting with objects, your commandos make noise. You can crouch (by holding the **Shift** key) to move silently, or use the environment to mask your movements, such as moving behind walls or through noisy areas where guards won't hear you.
- **Line of Sight**: Enemy guards have a limited line of sight. If you stay outside their field of view or remain behind cover, you can move

undetected. Be mindful of their patrol routes and timing to plan your movements accordingly.

- **Distractions**: One of the best ways to bypass enemies is by creating distractions. You can throw objects like rocks or cans to lure guards away from their posts. This allows your team to sneak past without being seen.

2. Tactical Movement

Tactical movement is about positioning your units for maximum advantage while avoiding detection and making the most of your commando's skills. Here's how you can utilize it effectively:

- **Moving Between Cover**: Always move from cover to cover. Whether it's behind a box, wall, or vehicle, staying out of sight is crucial. Use the **Ctrl + 1-6** shortcut to select multiple commandos and move them to their optimal positions without alerting enemies.
- **Overwatch and Ambushes**: Position your snipers and other ranged characters in elevated positions where they can observe enemy movements without being spotted. Setting up ambushes, where enemies are lured into vulnerable spots, is another powerful tactic.
- **Slow and Steady**: Sometimes, rushing into a mission is tempting, but it's better to take your time. Slow and steady movement allows you to assess the battlefield and reposition when necessary. Use the **Shift** key to move slowly and avoid being heard.

3. Coordination of Multiple Units

In *Commandos: Origins*, managing multiple characters is essential for success. Each commando brings something different to the table, and understanding how to use them in tandem will improve your tactical approach:

- **Group Commands**: Group your commandos together by holding **Ctrl + 1-6**. This allows you to move your team as a cohesive unit, making it easier to execute synchronized attacks or movements.
- **Simultaneous Actions**: When you need to issue multiple commands at once, use the **Shift** key to queue actions. For example, you can have one commando throw a rock to distract an enemy while another commando prepares for an ambush.

- **Line Formation**: Position your commandos in a line or staggered formation, ensuring that one unit's line of sight covers another's blind spots. This is particularly useful when preparing to breach enemy strongholds.

4. Using the Terrain to Your Advantage

The terrain in *Commandos: Origins* plays a pivotal role in your tactics. Not only does it provide cover and concealment, but it also offers opportunities to set traps or plan attacks:

- **Elevated Positions**: Placing your sniper or long-range characters on rooftops, hills, or balconies gives them a clear view of enemy movements. Elevation helps with both attack and observation.
- **Choke Points**: Narrow passages, such as doorways, bridges, and hallways, are perfect places to ambush enemies. By controlling these choke points, you can eliminate threats before they even get close.
- **Environmental Hazards**: The game's environment isn't just for cover; it also has interactive elements. Use explosive barrels to eliminate groups of enemies, or set off traps to create chaos among enemy ranks.

5. Managing Enemy Awareness

Your goal is to control the battlefield without being noticed, and enemy awareness plays a key part in that. Every time a guard spots you or hears something suspicious, their alert level increases. Here's how to keep enemy awareness low:

- **Avoiding Detection**: Ensure that your commandos stay out of enemy sightlines and avoid making noise by crouching or moving behind obstacles. If a guard starts moving toward you, it's time to retreat into cover.
- **Changing Routes**: If one path is heavily guarded, reroute your commandos. *Commandos: Origins* offers multiple ways to reach an objective, so don't be afraid to try new paths when your current one is compromised.

2.3 COMBAT MECHANICS

While *Commandos: Origins* heavily emphasizes stealth and tactical movement, combat plays a crucial role when things inevitably go wrong. Understanding the game's combat mechanics will help you maximize your offensive capabilities and manage difficult situations. Combat requires careful timing, precision, and the strategic use of your commandos' unique abilities.

1. Types of Combat

Commandos: Origins features several forms of combat, each with distinct strategies and execution methods. Let's break them down:

- **Melee Combat**:
  The Green Beret is your primary commando for melee combat, using brute force to take down enemies silently. Melee attacks can be used to incapacitate enemies without drawing attention, making them perfect for stealthy takedowns.
    - o **Tip**: Always be mindful of enemy patrols before engaging in melee combat. Use your surroundings to stay hidden after taking down a guard, as other enemies may be nearby.
- **Ranged Combat**:
  The Sniper is best suited for long-range combat, allowing you to eliminate enemies from a distance without being detected. Ranged combat requires patience and precision, and it's often best when used in conjunction with stealth.
    - o **Tip**: Elevate your sniper on high ground or behind cover to give them a clear line of sight. Make sure to time your shots carefully, as firing too early may alert nearby enemies.
- **Firearms and Explosives**:
  The Marine and Sapper excel in firearms and explosives. These weapons are loud and can alert enemies to your presence, so they should be used strategically. The Marine's heavy weapons and the Sapper's explosive devices can turn the tide of battle, especially when fighting in open areas or engaging heavily armored foes.
    - o **Tip**: Use explosives to destroy enemy equipment or block pathways. Firearms are ideal for clearing rooms, but be aware of the noise they generate.
- **Throwing Objects**:
  In addition to weapons, commandos can throw objects, such as rocks, bricks, and cans, to distract enemies or create diversions.

o   **Tip**: Use the environment to find objects you can throw. A well-timed distraction can pull enemies away from their posts, allowing your team to advance unnoticed.

2. Combat Engagement

While it's often preferable to avoid combat through stealth, sometimes you'll have to engage directly. Here's how to handle combat situations effectively:

- **Surprise Attacks**:
  A well-timed surprise attack can give you the upper hand. Use your Sniper to take out distant threats, or ambush enemies with your Green Beret in close-quarters combat.
  - o   **Tip**: Before engaging, use the pause function to plan your attack, positioning your commandos for optimal effectiveness.
- **Covering Fire**:
  The Marine's firepower is excellent for covering fire, allowing other commandos to advance or reposition. If you're under heavy fire, use the Marine to suppress enemies, giving your other commandos time to regroup or make tactical moves.
  - o   **Tip**: Place the Marine in a spot where they can cover your other commandos without getting too close to enemy lines. This way, they can provide effective support while remaining safe.
- **Managing Ammo**:
  Ammo management is critical in combat situations. Running out of bullets mid-fight can leave you vulnerable. Fortunately, there are opportunities to resupply during missions, but you'll need to be mindful of how many shots you take.
  - o   **Tip**: Conserve ammunition by using stealth and non-lethal methods whenever possible. If you must engage in combat, aim for headshots to reduce ammo usage.
- **Weapon Switching**:
  Switching between weapons and items is crucial during combat. The game allows you to quickly switch from a sniper rifle to a sidearm or explosive, depending on the situation.
  - o   **Tip**: Familiarize yourself with the weapon wheel or hotkeys to swiftly switch between weapons during combat. The quicker you can adapt to changing circumstances, the better.

3. Managing Enemy Awareness

Combat in *Commandos: Origins* doesn't just rely on brute force; managing enemy awareness is just as crucial. Here's how to control the battlefield:

- **Alert Status**:
  When an enemy spots you or hears a loud noise, their alert status will increase. If the alert level becomes too high, reinforcements will arrive, making the situation much harder to manage.
  - **Tip**: After an engagement, retreat to a safer location to reset the enemy's alert status. If you're spotted during an ambush, quickly reposition and eliminate the threat before the situation escalates.
- **Using the Environment**:
  Use objects and structures to your advantage. Taking cover behind walls or using terrain to block enemy line-of-sight will help you survive longer in combat. Environmental hazards like explosive barrels or electric fences can also be used against enemies.
  - **Tip**: Always scout the environment for potential hazards you can use against the enemy. If you can cause environmental damage, it's a good way to weaken the enemy before engaging directly.

2.4 MANAGING RESOURCES AND INVENTORY

In *Commandos: Origins*, managing resources and your inventory is essential for keeping your squad prepared for every mission. From ammunition to health packs, each item can be a lifesaver when used correctly.

1. Inventory System

Each commando in your squad has their own inventory, where they can store weapons, tools, and items found during the mission. The size of each commando's inventory is limited, so it's important to manage it wisely.

Item Type	Examples	Uses

Weapons	Pistols, Rifles, Sniper Rifles, Shotguns	Offensive tools for combat. Each commando can carry a limited number of weapons.
Tools	Lockpicks, Gas Masks, Rope	Special tools for specific tasks, such as unlocking doors or surviving hazardous environments.
Medical Supplies	First Aid Kits, Bandages	Used to heal injured commandos and restore health.
Explosives	Dynamite, Grenades, Mines	Useful for sabotaging enemy equipment or clearing paths.
Ammunition	Bullets, Explosive Charges	Replenishes weapons or provides additional offensive power.

2. Collecting Items

Throughout the game, your commandos will come across various items scattered across the map, or they may drop from defeated enemies. Items are vital to your survival and mission success, and knowing when and how to collect them is crucial:

- **Looting Bodies**: After eliminating enemies, be sure to loot their bodies for any useful items. Weapons, ammo, and medical supplies can often be found on fallen enemies.
- **Hidden Supplies**: Look for hidden supply caches or dropped items during exploration. These could include rare weapons, explosives, or health packs that will make future missions easier.

3. Managing Inventory Space

Each commando has limited space for items. You'll need to prioritize what they carry:

- **Only Pack What's Needed**: Avoid overloading your commandos with unnecessary items. A commando can only carry a limited amount of ammunition, weapons, and tools, so prioritize what's most useful for the mission at hand.

- **Drop or Transfer Items**: If you need to clear space for new items, you can drop them on the ground or transfer them to another commando. Be mindful, as some items can be dropped in vulnerable spots, leaving them exposed to enemies.

4. Health and Healing

Health management is vital for success in *Commandos: Origins*. If your commandos are injured, you'll need to quickly heal them using available medical supplies:

- **First Aid Kits**: These items heal a commando's health when they are low. Keep a few kits on hand for emergencies, as healing in the middle of combat can be the difference between life and death.
- **Bandages**: These can be used for smaller injuries or to prevent further health loss after an injury. Use them to stabilize your team before they are able to find more substantial medical supplies.

5. Using Items Strategically

Items like explosives, traps, and distractions can be incredibly useful when used at the right moment. Here's how to use them effectively:

- **Explosives**: Dynamite and grenades can clear obstacles or eliminate groups of enemies. Use them when stealth is no longer an option, or to destroy enemy equipment and structures.
- **Distraction Tools**: Use objects like rocks and cans to distract enemies. Throw them into different areas to lure enemies away from their patrol routes or to set up ambushes.

6. Ammunition Management

Ammunition is a finite resource, so managing your supply is critical, especially for characters like the Marine and Sniper, who rely heavily on firearms:

- **Conserve Ammo**: Use your weapons efficiently, aiming for headshots when possible to conserve ammunition. If a commando is running low on ammo, consider switching to a different commando or using explosives to reduce reliance on firearms.

- **Resupply**: Keep an eye out for supply caches or dropped ammo during missions. Running out of ammo at the wrong time can leave your commandos vulnerable.

CHAPTER 3: CHARACTER CLASSES AND ROLES

3.1 THE GREEN BERET: YOUR ALL-ROUNDER

In *Commandos: Origins*, the key to success lies in how you utilize your team of elite commandos, each with their own specialized skills and roles. Understanding these unique abilities and how to leverage them effectively will allow you to tackle a wide variety of mission objectives, whether it's silently infiltrating enemy territory or laying waste to enemy forces. This chapter will introduce you to two of the most important commandos in your squad: The Green Beret and The Sniper. Both are essential to your success, and mastering their abilities is crucial to completing your missions with precision.

The Green Beret is the ultimate versatile commando, capable of handling a wide range of tasks that make him invaluable in almost any situation. Whether you're in the midst of a firefight, trying to sneak past enemy patrols, or carrying out an important mission objective, the Green Beret is your go-to soldier. His combination of combat proficiency and utility allows him to adapt to a wide variety of roles, making him one of the most important assets in your team.

Key Abilities and Strengths

- **Hand-to-Hand Combat**:
  The Green Beret is an expert in close-quarters combat. He can take down enemies silently without raising an alarm. His skill in melee combat makes him ideal for taking out lone guards or infiltrating enemy positions without using weapons.
  - **Tip**: Use the Green Beret to incapacitate enemies quietly. When facing multiple enemies, use distractions (like throwing rocks) to lure guards away from their posts and eliminate them silently.
- **Carrying and Lifting Objects**:
  The Green Beret has the strength to carry heavy objects such as crates, barrels, and even dead bodies. This ability is especially useful when you need to hide or move large items without alerting the enemy.

o   **Tip**: If you need to hide a body to avoid enemy detection, the Green Beret can carry it to a safe spot. Additionally, his ability to move heavy objects can help clear blocked paths or provide additional cover.

- **Explosives Handling**:
  While not as skilled as the Sapper, the Green Beret is still capable of handling explosives for sabotage and combat purposes. He can plant or throw explosives in strategic locations to disrupt enemy formations or destroy key structures.

  o   **Tip**: Use the Green Beret for tactical explosive placements, such as disabling enemy vehicles or blowing up entry points when stealth is no longer an option.

- **Weapon Versatility**:
  In combat, the Green Beret is proficient with a wide array of weapons, including rifles, pistols, and shotguns. While he excels in melee, his gunplay can be relied upon when necessary.

  o   **Tip**: The Green Beret is a jack-of-all-trades, so use him in situations that require a quick transition between stealth and combat. His flexibility makes him ideal for handling unexpected threats.

How to Use the Green Beret Effectively

The Green Beret's versatility makes him perfect for almost any mission, but his best use comes from balancing both his combat and tactical abilities. Use him in situations that require a mix of combat and stealth, such as when you need to break through enemy lines or silently eliminate guards in your way.

- **Mid-Range Combat**: While the Sniper excels at long-range kills, the Green Beret is perfect for medium-range encounters. Use him to clear a path or provide cover fire when you need to make a quick escape or retreat.
- **Stealthy Sabotage**: The Green Beret's ability to carry and lift objects makes him an excellent candidate for sabotaging enemy operations without being detected. Move objects or bodies to obscure enemy vision or set up traps to hinder their progress.

The Green Beret's Role in Team Coordination

While the Green Beret is adaptable, coordinating him with other commandos is essential for maximum effectiveness. Pair him with stealthier characters like the Spy for infiltration or with the Marine for direct combat support when you need to clear enemy positions. His ability to move bodies and objects can also be vital when working with the Sniper to secure vantage points or set up ambushes.

3.2 THE SNIPER: MASTER OF LONG-RANGE ELIMINATION

The Sniper is the silent, deadly force in your team, capable of eliminating threats from a distance with precision and efficiency. When stealth is the key to mission success, the Sniper is indispensable. His ability to take out high-value targets without alerting the rest of the enemy forces allows your team to maintain control of the battlefield without compromising your position.

Key Abilities and Strengths

- **Long-Range Precision**:
  The Sniper's most notable strength is his long-range shooting ability. With a sniper rifle, he can eliminate enemies from great distances, often taking out guards before they even know what hit them.
  - **Tip**: Always find high ground or concealed positions for your Sniper to maximize his range and minimize the risk of detection. The higher the vantage point, the better the visibility and effectiveness of his shots.
- **One-Shot, One-Kill**:
  The Sniper is a master of headshots. A single well-placed shot can eliminate an enemy, often without alerting others. However, this requires patience and careful timing, as shooting too early or missing can compromise your position.
  - **Tip**: Use the pause feature to carefully line up your shots. Consider the wind, terrain, and enemy movements before firing to ensure that your shot is successful.
- **Silent Elimination**:
  The Sniper excels at silent eliminations. His rifle is designed to make minimal noise, allowing him to take out enemies without raising the alarm. This is crucial for missions where stealth is paramount.

- o **Tip**: Take out high-priority targets (such as guards near important objectives) with the Sniper, as his ability to operate without being detected can make him invaluable for clearing paths.
- **Spotting Enemies**:
  In addition to eliminating threats, the Sniper can spot enemies at a distance and provide valuable intel to your team. By scouting out enemy positions, he helps you plan your next move and anticipate threats.
  - o **Tip**: Before engaging in combat, use the Sniper to scan the battlefield. His keen eyesight allows him to spot enemies and obstacles that other commandos may miss.

How to Use the Sniper Effectively

The Sniper excels in specific situations, where a well-placed shot can shift the momentum of the mission. His role is to clear out targets that pose a significant threat while the rest of the team moves in for other objectives. Here's how to use him to his fullest potential:

- **Long-Distance Engagements**: When dealing with enemy guards positioned at distant vantage points, have the Sniper take them out from afar. This allows the rest of your team to move freely without the risk of being detected.
- **Covering Stealth Operations**: Pair the Sniper with the Spy or Green Beret to provide cover for their movements. The Sniper can eliminate guards from a distance, allowing your stealthier team members to infiltrate enemy positions with minimal risk.

The Sniper's Role in Team Coordination

The Sniper is at his best when working in tandem with other commandos. Use him to provide support for other members of the team, especially when clearing enemy positions or taking out high-value targets. He excels in situations where a precise shot can neutralize a threat before it becomes a problem.

- **Complementing the Green Beret**: While the Green Beret is capable of direct combat, the Sniper can eliminate enemies before they get close enough to pose a threat. Pairing these two commandos allows you to clear paths and eliminate obstacles from a distance.

- **Assisting with Ambushes**: Position the Sniper at a strategic location where he can take out enemy reinforcements or backup. A single well-placed shot can turn the tide of battle, especially when the Sniper provides support from a hidden vantage point.

3.3 THE SAPPER: EXPERT IN DEMOLITIONS

The Sapper is a vital commando in *Commandos: Origins*, specializing in explosives, sabotage, and strategic demolitions. While he may not be as versatile in direct combat as the Green Beret or as precise as the Sniper, his ability to deal with obstacles, set traps, and destroy critical enemy infrastructure is unmatched. The Sapper is essential for any mission that involves sabotaging enemy resources, clearing paths, or causing chaos behind enemy lines.

Key Abilities and Strengths

- **Explosives Handling**:
  The Sapper is the only commando capable of handling and deploying explosives with precision. He can plant dynamite, set mines, and detonate enemy vehicles, making him invaluable when it comes to creating diversions or eliminating high-value targets.
    o **Tip**: Use the Sapper's explosives to destroy enemy vehicles or key infrastructure, such as bridges or communication towers. Timing is critical when setting up these charges, so ensure the area is clear before detonation.
- **Minefield Clearing**:
  Mines and other explosive traps are common in enemy territory. The Sapper can safely disarm or disable these traps, allowing your team to move through potentially hazardous areas.
    o **Tip**: Always bring the Sapper when you suspect mines or explosives are present. His skill in disabling these devices will help prevent unnecessary losses.
- **Sabotaging Enemy Equipment**:
  The Sapper excels at sabotaging enemy equipment, whether it's disabling turrets, destroying enemy supplies, or causing critical damage to enemy structures. His ability to neutralize enemy assets without direct combat is crucial for stealthy missions.

- ○ **Tip**: When you need to cause disruption behind enemy lines, the Sapper is your go-to commando. Use him to disable or destroy enemy weaponry, transport, and key objectives without alerting the rest of the force.
- **Trap Setting**:
  The Sapper can set traps for unsuspecting enemies, such as explosive traps or trigger points that activate upon movement. These traps can cause chaos and disorient enemies, making it easier for your team to take control of the situation.
  - ○ **Tip**: Lay explosive traps along patrol routes or near enemy strongholds to catch enemies off guard. The Sapper's traps can create openings for other commandos to infiltrate or advance.

How to Use the Sapper Effectively

The Sapper is best used in situations where explosives or sabotage are required to complete objectives or create diversions. Here's how to make the most of his abilities:

- **Clearing Enemy Structures**: Use the Sapper to destroy key enemy infrastructure like supply depots, vehicles, or defensive positions. These actions will weaken the enemy's hold on the area, making it easier for the rest of your squad to complete the mission.
- **Creating Diversions**: Place explosive charges near enemy patrol routes to create distractions. The noise and chaos will draw enemy forces away from their positions, allowing your team to move or attack without being detected.
- **Mine Removal**: Always send the Sapper into potentially dangerous areas with mines. His expertise will ensure your team can navigate without taking casualties from explosive traps.

The Sapper's Role in Team Coordination

The Sapper's primary role is to disrupt and destroy, and he works best when paired with other commandos. His ability to clear paths and disable enemy forces allows the rest of your team to operate with more freedom:

- **Paired with the Green Beret**: Use the Sapper in conjunction with the Green Beret for silent infiltration and destruction. While the

Green Beret takes care of enemy guards, the Sapper can plant explosives or disable traps ahead of the team.

- **Coordinating with the Marine**: If you're about to assault a heavily guarded enemy base, the Sapper can take out key defensive positions, such as turrets and vehicles, while the Marine provides heavy fire support.

3.4 THE SPY: STEALTH AND DECEPTION

The Spy is the ultimate master of stealth and deception in *Commandos: Origins*. His ability to blend in with enemy forces and gather intelligence makes him one of the most powerful commandos in the game, especially when your mission relies on subtlety and precision. Unlike other commandos, the Spy excels at infiltration, gathering information, and sabotaging enemy operations from within without ever revealing his presence.

Key Abilities and Strengths

- **Disguise and Blending In**:
  The Spy's ability to disguise himself as enemy personnel is one of his most valuable skills. He can wear enemy uniforms to infiltrate enemy bases, pass unnoticed through enemy ranks, and gather vital intelligence.
  - o **Tip**: Always use the Spy to infiltrate enemy positions, especially when you need to gather information or reach areas that are heavily guarded. His disguise allows him to bypass enemy patrols and enter restricted areas undetected.
- **Unlocking Doors and Chests**:
  The Spy can unlock doors and safes, making him essential for accessing restricted areas or retrieving valuable intel. Whether it's a high-security building or a locked container, the Spy's lockpicking skills are invaluable.
  - o **Tip**: Use the Spy to access enemy offices, safehouses, or weapon caches. His ability to unlock doors can also help you find hidden documents or maps that will provide important mission information.
- **Sabotage from Within**:
  The Spy can sabotage enemy equipment, such as disabling communication devices, cutting power supplies, or even poisoning

food or water sources. His subtle approach means he can do these tasks without ever raising suspicion.

- o **Tip**: Use the Spy for covert sabotage when you need to cause disruption within enemy ranks. His abilities allow you to weaken the enemy without ever firing a shot or being seen.

- **Gathering   Intelligence**:
  The Spy excels at gathering information that can give your team a strategic advantage. Whether it's reading enemy communications, eavesdropping on conversations, or stealing classified documents, the Spy is crucial for missions that require careful intelligence gathering.
  - o **Tip**: Have the Spy gather critical intel before launching a full assault. He can provide information about enemy locations, patrol patterns, and hidden objectives that will give your team the upper hand.

How to Use the Spy Effectively

The Spy's strengths lie in his ability to blend in with enemies, infiltrate enemy lines, and gather information. Here's how to use him to his fullest potential:

- **Infiltrating Enemy Bases**: The Spy is perfect for missions that require you to sneak into enemy bases without raising alarms. Use him to scout the area, gather intel, or disable enemy defenses from within.
- **Sabotage and Distraction**: The Spy's ability to sabotage enemy equipment without being detected makes him ideal for creating distractions. Disabling enemy communications or triggering false alarms can confuse the enemy, giving your team the opportunity to move in or strike.
- **Stealthy Objective Completion**: When your mission requires the completion of objectives without direct combat, the Spy is invaluable. Use him to unlock doors, collect documents, or disable security systems in critical areas.

The Spy's Role in Team Coordination

While the Spy operates mostly alone, his actions directly impact the success of your entire team. Here's how to coordinate him with the rest of your squad:

- **Pairing with the Sniper**: The Spy's ability to gather intel and infiltrate enemy positions is perfect when paired with the Sniper. The Sniper can cover the Spy from a distance, picking off enemies as the Spy moves through the enemy ranks.
- **Supporting the Green Beret**: The Spy's disguises and stealth abilities complement the Green Beret's combat skills. Use the Spy to infiltrate a base, gather intel, and disable security measures, while the Green Beret clears the way or handles enemy encounters.

CHAPTER 4: WEAPONS AND EQUIPMENT

4.1 OVERVIEW OF AVAILABLE WEAPONS

In *Commandos: Origins*, having the right weapon or tool for the job is just as important as having the right commando. Each mission presents unique challenges, and your success depends on your ability to manage your resources effectively, particularly weapons and equipment. This chapter will cover the different types of weapons and equipment available in the game, helping you understand how to choose and use them strategically to achieve your mission goals.

Weapons in *Commandos: Origins* are your primary means of dealing with enemy forces. Each commando has access to a set of specific weapons that suit their skills and role. Understanding the different types of weapons and their functions is crucial to mastering combat in the game. Below is an overview of the primary weapon types you'll encounter:

Weapon Type	Description	Best Use
Pistols	Lightweight, quick-firing sidearms. Offers moderate accuracy and damage but low range.	Ideal for quick, close-range encounters and stealthy eliminations.
Rifles	Standard long-range weapons with a high damage output. Can be used for precise shots.	Best for mid-range combat and supporting snipers.
Sniper Rifles	Long-range, high-accuracy weapons capable of eliminating enemies from great distances.	Perfect for picking off enemies from hidden vantage points.

Shotguns	Short-range, high-damage weapons with a wide spread. Effective in close quarters.	Use when you need to clear rooms or deal with clustered enemies.
Submachine Guns	Fast-firing, automatic weapons with moderate accuracy.	Best for close to medium-range combat where high volume of fire is needed.
Grenades	Throwable explosives that deal area damage.	Useful for clearing enemy clusters or destroying obstacles.
Dynamite	Large explosive charges that can destroy structures or large groups of enemies.	Perfect for sabotaging enemy infrastructure or causing chaos.
Melee Weapons	Knives, crowbars, and other close-range tools used for silent takedowns.	Ideal for stealthy, non-lethal takedowns.

Weapon Categories and Their Purpose

- **Melee Weapons**:
  Melee weapons are essential for silent, close-range engagements. They are the go-to choice for taking out enemies quietly without alerting others to your presence. The Green Beret excels at using these weapons to incapacitate enemies swiftly.
- **Firearms**:
  Firearms come in various forms, each designed for different situations. Sniper rifles are used for long-range precision, while shotguns and submachine guns are better suited for mid-to-close combat. Choosing the right firearm depends on the range and type of engagement you expect.
- **Explosives**:
  Explosives such as grenades and dynamite are used for creating chaos, breaking through enemy defenses, or eliminating large groups of enemies. However, their use is noisy, so you'll want to use them sparingly and with discretion.

4.2 MELEE WEAPONS VS. FIREARMS: WHEN TO USE THEM

Choosing between melee weapons and firearms depends on the situation, and knowing when to use one over the other can greatly influence the outcome of a mission. Both types of weapons have their advantages and drawbacks, and understanding these will help you make better tactical decisions on the battlefield.

Melee Weapons: When to Use Them

Melee weapons are designed for silent takedowns, allowing your team to deal with enemies without alerting the rest of the enemy forces. The Green Beret, in particular, is skilled in using melee weapons for close combat.

Advantages of Melee Weapons:

- **Silence**: Melee weapons produce no sound, making them perfect for stealthy eliminations. This allows you to eliminate enemies without raising alarm or alerting nearby guards.
- **Precision**: A well-executed melee takedown can be just as effective as a firearm shot, especially if done from behind or when the enemy is unaware.
- **No Ammunition Required**: Melee weapons don't require ammo, which is a significant advantage in long missions where ammo may be scarce.

When to Use Melee Weapons:

- **Stealth Operations**: When you need to eliminate guards silently without alerting others, melee weapons are your best choice. They're essential for missions that rely heavily on discretion.
- **Close-Quarters Combat**: If you're in tight spaces like narrow hallways or small rooms, melee weapons can be more effective than firearms, allowing for quick eliminations.
- **Resource Management**: Melee weapons don't consume ammunition, so use them when you want to conserve ammo for more crucial situations.

Limitations of Melee Weapons:

- **Limited Range**: Melee weapons are only useful when you're close to the enemy. You'll need to get up close and personal, which may not always be feasible or safe, especially if there are multiple enemies.
- **Vulnerability**: Engaging in melee combat puts you at greater risk of being noticed, especially if the area isn't well-concealed or if the enemy has backup nearby.

Firearms: When to Use Them

Firearms offer a range of advantages, particularly when you need to engage enemies at medium to long distances. Whether it's the Sniper picking off a distant target or the Marine using a shotgun to clear a room, firearms are essential tools in your arsenal.

Advantages of Firearms:

- **Longer Range**: Firearms like rifles and sniper rifles allow you to engage enemies from a distance, providing safety and strategic advantages. This is perfect when you need to eliminate a target without getting too close.
- **High Damage Output**: Firearms tend to deliver much higher damage compared to melee weapons, especially in combat situations where multiple enemies are present.
- **Variety of Options**: With different types of firearms available, you can choose between a sniper rifle for precision, a submachine gun for rapid fire, or a shotgun for close-range, high-damage combat.

When to Use Firearms:

- **Long-Range Engagement**: Use firearms like sniper rifles for eliminating enemies from a distance, where stealth is no longer possible. The Sniper is particularly effective in this role.
- **Medium to Close-Range Combat**: For confrontations where you're under pressure or surrounded by enemies, firearms like shotguns and submachine guns are ideal. They provide rapid fire and can clear out enemies quickly.
- **Ambushes and Open Combat**: Firearms are perfect when stealth is no longer viable, and you need to fight your way out. The Green Beret or Marine can engage enemies head-on with shotguns or assault rifles.

Limitations of Firearms:

- **Noise**: Firearms generate noise, which alerts nearby enemies to your position. This makes them less effective in stealth-based missions, where silence is critical.
- **Ammunition Usage**: Firearms consume ammunition, and if you're not careful, you might find yourself running out at the worst possible time. Managing your ammo is vital during longer missions.

Firearms vs. Melee: Choosing the Right Tool for the Job

The decision between melee and firearms often comes down to the mission's objectives and the situation at hand. Here's a quick guide to help you choose the right weapon:

Scenario	Best Weapon Choice	Reason
Stealthy Infiltration	Melee Weapons	Silent takedowns prevent enemy awareness and allow for undetected movement.
Long-Range Elimination	Sniper Rifle	Precision kills from a distance, without alerting enemies.
Clearing Tight Spaces or Rooms	Shotgun	High damage output in confined spaces, perfect for dealing with groups.
Multiple Enemies in Open Combat	Submachine Gun or Assault Rifle	High fire rate and damage to take down groups of enemies.
Disrupting Enemy Operations	Explosives (Grenades, Dynamite)	Causing chaos, destroying equipment, and taking out multiple enemies.

Handling Close-Quarter Threats	Melee Weapons or Shotgun	Close-range engagement without wasting ammunition.

4.3 SPECIAL EQUIPMENT AND GADGETS

In *Commandos: Origins*, your success doesn't solely depend on weapons special equipment and gadgets play a crucial role in completing objectives, gathering intel, and avoiding detection. These tools are designed to provide unique advantages in specific situations, making them indispensable for certain missions. This section will cover the special equipment and gadgets available in the game, highlighting their uses and when to incorporate them into your strategy.

1. Lockpicks

Description:
Lockpicks are essential tools for gaining access to locked doors, safes, and other secured locations. The Spy is the primary commando for using lockpicks, but any character can use them if needed. They are especially useful for stealthy operations where avoiding detection is critical.

Best Use:

- **Infiltration**: Use lockpicks to unlock doors and gain access to restricted areas.
- **Information Gathering**: Some areas, such as enemy offices or storage rooms, may contain valuable documents or supplies that will help you achieve mission objectives.

Tip: Always check the map for locked doors or safes, as these often contain hidden intel or mission-critical items.

2. Gas Mask

Description:
The gas mask is an essential item when dealing with chemical warfare or toxic environments. Some areas in *Commandos: Origins* feature gas-filled rooms or toxic clouds that will kill or incapacitate your team without

protection. The Spy can carry the gas mask, enabling him to pass through these areas safely.

Best Use:

- **Toxic Zones**: When you encounter areas filled with gas or toxic fumes, equip your team with gas masks to avoid taking damage.
- **Stealthy Passage**: The Spy can use the gas mask to access areas that others can't, such as enemy facilities contaminated with chemical agents.

Tip: Use gas masks strategically ensure that only those who need it have one, as carrying unnecessary items can reduce inventory space.

3. Binoculars

Description:
Binoculars are a useful reconnaissance tool, allowing your team to spot enemies, objectives, or hidden areas from a distance. The Sniper often carries binoculars to help survey the battlefield before taking shots, but other commandos can also use them to spot enemies outside of their line of sight.

Best Use:

- **Reconnaissance**: Before entering an area, use binoculars to scout enemy positions, patrol routes, and possible obstacles.
- **Spotting Key Targets**: The Sniper can use binoculars to spot distant targets, making long-range eliminations easier.

Tip: Position your Sniper or other commandos in a safe, elevated position to use binoculars for a broader view of the battlefield.

4. Rope and Hook

Description:
The rope and hook are perfect for scaling walls, fences, or buildings. The Sapper and Spy are equipped with this tool, allowing them to reach higher or otherwise inaccessible areas without needing to go through guarded entrances.

Best Use:

- **Climbing Obstacles**: Use the rope to climb walls, fences, or any vertical obstacle that might block your way.
- **Escape Routes**: If your team is spotted and you need to retreat, the rope can provide an escape route by climbing to higher ground or entering hidden areas.

Tip: Use the rope and hook when you need to access rooftops or ledges that provide a tactical advantage, especially for your Sniper or Spy.

5. Flashbangs

Description:
Flashbangs are non-lethal grenades that temporarily blind and disorient enemies within a small radius. When deployed effectively, they can incapacitate guards, allowing your team to move past or eliminate them without raising an alarm.

Best Use:

- **Distraction and Diversion**: Flashbangs are perfect for disorienting enemies during ambushes, providing your team with an opportunity to strike or escape.
- **Room Clears**: Use flashbangs when entering rooms or bunkers with multiple enemies. The blinding effect gives your team the upper hand in combat.

Tip: Flashbangs work best when used strategically in confined spaces, where their disorienting effect can neutralize multiple enemies at once.

6. Cameras and Motion Sensors

Description:
Cameras and motion sensors are used by enemies to monitor and detect intruders. While these gadgets are used by the opposition, you can also use them to your advantage. The Sapper is capable of disabling these devices, while the Spy can avoid their detection by taking the necessary precautions.

Best Use:

- **Disabling Security**: Use the Sapper to disable cameras and motion sensors, creating a safe path for your team.
- **Stealth Avoidance**: The Spy can avoid cameras and motion sensors by using cover and staying out of sight, ensuring he remains undetected.

Tip: Before engaging in any mission, assess the area for security systems. Disable them early to avoid setting off alarms and alerting nearby enemies.

4.4 BEST LOADOUTS FOR EACH MISSION

Choosing the right loadout for each mission is critical to success. Depending on the mission's objectives and the environment, certain weapons and equipment will be more effective than others. In this section, we'll look at the best loadouts for different types of missions in *Commandos: Origins*, ensuring that you're always prepared for whatever lies ahead.

Mission Type	Recommended Loadout	Reason
Stealth Infiltration	Spy (Disguise, Lockpicks, Gas Mask), Green Beret (Melee Weapon), Sniper (Rifle, Binoculars)	Ideal for sneaking past enemies and gathering intel. Stealth is key, so use non-lethal weapons and the Spy's disguise to remain undetected.
Sabotage and Demolition	Sapper (Dynamite, Explosives, Rope), Green Beret (Melee Weapon, Shotgun)	Use the Sapper for disabling equipment and planting explosives. The Green Beret provides backup for close-quarters combat and defending against enemies.
Ambush and Assault	Marine (Assault Rifle, Shotgun), Sniper (Sniper Rifle), Green Beret (Submachine Gun, Melee)	Best for direct combat. The Marine's firepower can suppress enemies, while the Sniper picks off targets from a distance. The Green Beret handles close-range engagements.

Recon and Intelligence Gathering	Spy (Disguise, Binoculars), Sniper (Sniper Rifle, Binoculars), Green Beret (Melee)	The Spy infiltrates enemy lines and gathers intel while the Sniper provides cover. The Green Beret ensures close-quarter security when needed.
Rescue Operation	Green Beret (Melee, Shotgun), Marine (Submachine Gun), Sapper (Rope)	The Green Beret clears paths, while the Marine provides heavy fire support. The Sapper ensures access to high-security areas via rope and hook.
Escape and Evade	Green Beret (Melee, Shotgun), Spy (Disguise, Lockpicks), Sniper (Rifle)	The Green Beret clears a safe route for escape, while the Spy provides cover through disguises and lockpicks. The Sniper ensures a safe passage by eliminating distant threats.

General Loadout Tips:

- **Stealth Missions**: Always prioritize silence and stealth. Equip your Spy with a disguise and lockpicks, and the Green Beret with a melee weapon. Avoid firearms and explosives unless absolutely necessary.
- **Combat Missions**: If a mission demands more direct combat, focus on firepower. Equip your Marine with a submachine gun or shotgun and back him up with the Sniper for long-range support.
- **Demolition/Disruption**: Equip the Sapper with explosives and the Green Beret with heavy weapons. You'll need to cause chaos quickly, so having explosive tools at the ready is crucial.
- **Recon and Intelligence**: Prioritize tools that help you gather information. The Spy's disguise and lockpicks are essential, along with binoculars for spotting enemies and objectives from a distance.

CHAPTER 5: STRATEGIES AND TIPS

5.1 MASTERING STEALTH TACTICS

Mastering the core mechanics in *Commandos: Origins* is only part of the journey. The key to completing missions efficiently and successfully lies in your ability to think strategically and use the game's systems to your advantage. This chapter dives into some of the most effective strategies, focusing on stealth tactics and how to manipulate the environment to create opportunities and overcome challenges.

Stealth is one of the most crucial aspects of *Commandos: Origins*, and it's essential to your success in most missions. Whether you're infiltrating an enemy base, gathering intel, or taking out guards without raising an alarm, knowing how to operate under the radar will make all the difference. This section covers the essential techniques for mastering stealth tactics and how to avoid detection while achieving your objectives.

1. Use Silence to Your Advantage

The key to stealth in *Commandos: Origins* is to avoid making noise. Every action you take whether it's moving, interacting with objects, or attacking enemies can alert the guards to your presence. Here are some ways to minimize noise:

- **Move Slowly**: Always move your commandos slowly by holding down the **Shift** key. This reduces the noise they make, helping them stay hidden from nearby enemies.
- **Crouch for Extra Stealth**: When moving through areas with close enemies, crouching will further reduce the noise. Crouching is essential when you're sneaking past patrols or avoiding detection in high-alert areas.
- **Avoid Running**: Running is a dead giveaway to the enemy. Only sprint when absolutely necessary and when you're sure there's no immediate risk of being seen.
- **Listen for Audio Cues**: Pay attention to the audio cues around you. Enemy dialogue, footsteps, and the environment itself can provide clues about patrol routes and areas of danger.

2. Avoiding Enemy Sightlines

Every enemy in *Commandos: Origins* has a line of sight that you need to manage. Moving within their sight radius will alert them, leading to combat or the calling of reinforcements. Here's how to stay out of sight:

- **Stay in the Shadows**: Make use of shadows, walls, and objects to hide from enemies. Most enemies won't notice you as long as you stay out of their direct line of sight.
- **Use Cover**: Objects such as crates, barrels, and vehicles provide great cover. Move from one piece of cover to another, avoiding open spaces where enemies can see you.
- **Monitor Patrols**: Enemy patrols will often follow predictable paths. Take the time to observe their movements and time your movements accordingly. You can use the pause function to plan your next steps if you're unsure of an enemy's location.

3. Take Out Enemies Quietly

There will be times when you need to eliminate enemies to clear the way for your team. Here's how to do it without alerting others:

- **Melee Takedowns**: The Green Beret is an expert at taking down enemies silently. Use melee takedowns whenever possible, especially when you need to eliminate a lone guard.
- **Non-Lethal Elimination**: Some enemies can be incapacitated without being killed. Use tools like chloroform or specific gadgets to quietly subdue enemies, leaving them unable to raise the alarm.
- **Body Disposal**: After taking down an enemy, always hide their body. The Green Beret can carry them out of sight, or you can use nearby cover to tuck them away. This prevents other guards from discovering the body and raising the alarm.

4. Use Distractions and Diversions

If you find yourself in a situation where it's impossible to avoid detection, distractions can help you regain the upper hand. *Commandos: Origins* offers several ways to create diversions:

- **Throw Objects**: Throwing rocks, bottles, or cans can distract enemies, pulling them away from their patrol routes or points of interest. This gives you the opportunity to move past them unnoticed.

- **Activate Noisy Objects**: If available, you can activate noisy objects like alarms or machines to create confusion and draw attention away from your team.
- **Use Flashbangs**: Flashbangs can temporarily blind enemies and cause disorientation, allowing you to either escape or silently eliminate them while they recover.

5.2 HOW TO USE THE ENVIRONMENT TO YOUR ADVANTAGE

In *Commandos: Origins*, the environment plays a vital role in how you approach every mission. You can use the environment to hide, create distractions, gain high ground, and even sabotage enemy operations. This section explores various ways to manipulate the environment to give you the edge over the enemy.

1. Elevation for Tactical Advantage

High ground offers several key advantages in *Commandos: Origins*. Whether it's providing a sniper with a clear line of sight or allowing a commando to move undetected, elevation can be a game-changer.

- **Sniper Vantage Points**: Position your Sniper on rooftops, hills, or elevated platforms for a broader view of the battlefield. This provides an advantage in spotting enemies and taking out distant targets without being detected.
- **Move Over Obstacles**: Use ladders, ropes, or stairs to access elevated areas. These routes can often bypass enemy patrols or avoid heavily guarded zones.
- **Ambush Opportunities**: Position your commandos in elevated locations to set up ambushes. Enemies who move into the area below can be picked off one by one without alerting others.

2. Using Cover and Concealment

The landscape is filled with opportunities for cover, but it's not just about staying out of sight. You also need to think about positioning and how you can manipulate the environment to avoid detection.

- **Behind Objects**: Use objects like walls, crates, and vehicles to stay hidden. If you need to cross open areas, always ensure there's cover nearby to duck behind if you're spotted.
- **Natural Obstacles**: Trees, rocks, and fences are ideal for hiding. Take note of how these natural barriers can help you move across the map while remaining unseen.
- **Creating Barriers**: In some cases, you can move or interact with objects to block enemy sightlines or create choke points. For instance, you can push a cart into a narrow passage to force enemies to detour or open a gate to create a physical barrier between you and pursuing forces.

3. Environmental Hazards

The environment itself can become a weapon. Many levels feature hazards you can exploit to your advantage, turning the terrain into an ally.

- **Explosive Barrels**: These barrels can be found throughout many levels and can be shot to create explosive hazards for your enemies. Set them up near enemy patrols or vehicles for devastating results.
- **Traps**: Mines, tripwires, and other traps are common in enemy territory. The Sapper is the best at disabling these traps, but you can also use them to your advantage by triggering them to take out large groups of enemies or block pathways.
- **Fire and Water**: In certain environments, fire hazards like torches or open flames can be used to set off explosions or burn enemies. Conversely, water can sometimes act as a way to bypass sections of the map or drown enemies by pushing them into bodies of water.

4. Sabotaging Enemy Equipment

Sometimes, it's not just about evading or engaging enemies directly it's about disrupting their operations. *Commandos: Origins* gives you the tools to sabotage enemy equipment and resources, crippling their ability to fight back or track your movements.

- **Disabling Vehicles**: Use the Sapper's explosives or the Spy's sabotage abilities to disable enemy vehicles. This prevents them from quickly reaching other areas and disrupts their supply lines.
- **Cutting Power**: If the area has electrical systems, the Spy can cut power to specific locations, leaving enemies in the dark. This opens

up new paths for your team or forces enemies into vulnerable positions.

- **Communications Sabotage**: Destroying communication equipment disables enemy coordination, making it harder for them to call reinforcements or alert other guards. The Spy is ideal for this kind of task, as his skills allow him to perform sabotage undetected.

5.3 TIMING AND PATIENCE: KEY TO SUCCESS

In *Commandos: Origins*, patience and precise timing are often the difference between success and failure. Unlike many action-heavy games, *Commandos: Origins* rewards slow, deliberate play where every move must be carefully considered. The key to success lies in waiting for the right moment to strike, planning your actions in advance, and maintaining a calm and steady pace throughout each mission.

1. Patience is Essential for Stealth

One of the most important aspects of *Commandos: Origins* is its emphasis on stealth. In order to avoid detection and remain undetected, patience is your best ally.

- **Wait for the Right Moment**: Enemies follow specific patrol routes, and it's crucial to wait until they move out of sight before you act. Premature actions, such as rushing through an area or making a move when an enemy is nearby, can quickly alert the guards, leading to disastrous consequences.
- **Take Time to Observe**: Before making a move, take the time to observe enemy patrols and their patterns. Knowing where the enemy is at all times will give you the opportunity to plan your actions and avoid dangerous situations.
- **Rest and Regroup**: If you're in a position where your team has been spotted or you're close to being detected, take a step back. Resetting and regaining your composure will allow you to reassess your strategy and plan for a more successful attempt.

2. Timing is Crucial for Combat Engagements

When combat becomes inevitable, timing your actions in *Commandos: Origins* can mean the difference between a quick win or a drawn-out, chaotic battle.

- **Wait for the Right Opening**: Don't rush into a fight. Wait for the enemy to be distracted or positioned in a way that maximizes your advantages. A well-timed attack can eliminate threats without drawing attention from other guards.
- **Coordinate Attacks**: If multiple commandos are engaged in combat, make sure they attack simultaneously or in sequence, ensuring no one is left exposed. This will prevent enemies from retaliating before they are neutralized.
- **Use the Pause Feature**: The ability to pause the game is a critical tool for timing. When things start to get tense or you're unsure of the next move, pause the game and plan ahead. This allows you to issue commands to all your commandos simultaneously, maximizing efficiency.

3. Don't Rush: Slow and Steady Wins the Mission

In *Commandos: Origins*, the best way to approach missions is with a slow, methodical mindset. Rushing through areas or attempting to force your way through challenges can lead to unnecessary mistakes. Instead, take your time and focus on making deliberate, calculated moves.

- **Observe Before Moving**: Always take a moment to scan the area before proceeding. Look for enemy patrols, obstacles, and potential routes. Don't just move because you can take the time to understand the environment first.
- **Double-Check Your Plan**: Before executing any action, double-check your plan. Is there another way to achieve the objective? Are there alternate routes or opportunities for stealth? Making sure your approach is solid before proceeding can save you from wasting resources or getting caught.

5.4 TEAM COORDINATION AND SYNERGY

While each commando in *Commandos: Origins* is skilled individually, the true strength of your team comes from how well you coordinate their efforts. Teamwork and synergy are vital to completing complex objectives, especially in situations where stealth is required. This section will explore the best strategies for coordinating your team and leveraging the unique abilities of each commando to ensure success.

1. Understanding Each Commando's Strengths

Each commando in *Commandos: Origins* brings something unique to the table. Understanding their abilities and roles within your team is crucial for coordinating effectively and maximizing the team's potential.

- **Green Beret**: The Green Beret is your all-around commando. He can engage in melee combat, carry heavy objects, and clear paths for your team. His versatility makes him ideal for a wide range of roles, from stealth to combat.
- **Sniper**: The Sniper is essential for long-range eliminations and overwatch. He excels at eliminating distant threats without alerting nearby enemies. Position him in high vantage points to cover the team while they move through dangerous areas.
- **Sapper**: The Sapper is your demolition expert, ideal for sabotaging enemy equipment and clearing obstacles. His ability to plant explosives and disarm traps makes him crucial for missions that require tactical disruption.
- **Spy**: The Spy is your stealth and deception specialist. He can blend in with enemies, gather intel, and sabotage equipment without raising suspicion. Use the Spy to infiltrate enemy lines and gather vital information or disable enemy defenses.
- **Marine**: The Marine is your heavy hitter. He's perfect for direct combat, using powerful firearms to take down enemies head-on. When things go south, the Marine's firepower can provide the backup you need to regroup or retreat.

2. Assigning Roles Based on Mission Objectives

The key to success lies in how you assign roles to your commandos based on the mission's specific objectives. A successful strategy requires knowing which commando to use for each task and how to combine their strengths to achieve the goal.

- **Stealth Missions**: For stealthy operations, assign the Spy to infiltrate enemy lines and gather intel. The Green Beret can be used for close-range takedowns, while the Sniper provides long-range cover. The Sapper should be used to disable enemy alarms or traps to keep the mission quiet.

- **Combat Missions**: When combat becomes unavoidable, the Marine should take the lead, using heavy weapons to suppress enemy fire. The Green Beret can assist in close combat, while the Sniper takes out distant threats from a safe distance.
- **Sabotage Missions**: For missions that require destruction or sabotage, the Sapper is your go-to commando. Have him plant explosives, disable vehicles, or sabotage enemy equipment. Meanwhile, use the Green Beret or Marine for backup in case things go wrong.

3. Synchronizing Actions for Maximum Efficiency

Effective coordination between your team members is key to achieving mission success. In *Commandos: Origins*, you can issue commands to all commandos at once, ensuring that everyone is on the same page and executing their actions simultaneously.

- **Simultaneous Movement**: Use the pause feature to plan coordinated movements for multiple commandos. For example, move the Spy into position to unlock a door while the Sniper covers him from a distance. Then, have the Green Beret and Marine move forward to eliminate any guards that might pose a threat.
- **Team Ambushes**: Set up ambushes by having commandos take positions in strategic locations. Use the Sniper to eliminate high-value targets from a distance, while the Green Beret and Marine engage enemies up close.
- **Timed Explosives**: When using explosives, ensure that all commandos are in a safe position before detonation. Have the Sapper plant explosives while the Green Beret and other team members position themselves to handle any remaining threats.

4. Communication is Key

While the game doesn't require direct communication like multiplayer games, the idea of coordinating actions between your team members is still vital. Always think of your commandos as part of a greater whole, with each member working toward a shared goal. Proper timing and planning are essential for overcoming obstacles and completing complex missions.

- **Reacting to Changing Situations**: Sometimes, unexpected events will force you to adapt on the fly. Whether it's a guard spotting one of your team members or an alarm going off, being able to quickly change your strategy and communicate with your team (using the pause function) will help you regain control.
- **Backup Plans**: Always have a backup plan in case things don't go as expected. If an ambush fails, have a contingency plan for getting your team out of trouble. This can mean switching to combat mode, using explosives to create diversions, or retreating to a safe position.

CHAPTER 6: MISSION WALKTHROUGHS

6.1 MISSION 1: THE BEGINNING OF THE WAR

In *Commandos: Origins*, each mission presents a unique challenge that requires careful planning, execution, and strategy. This chapter provides detailed walkthroughs for each mission in the game, breaking down the key objectives, potential obstacles, and the best strategies to succeed. Whether you're a seasoned player or a newcomer, these step-by-step guides will help you navigate even the most complex missions with ease.

Objective **Overview**

Mission 1: The Beginning of the War serves as both an introduction to the game's mechanics and a primer on the strategic elements you will need to master in future missions. In this mission, you'll be tasked with infiltrating an enemy outpost, gathering critical intel, and making your way to a safe extraction point. Although it's designed to ease you into the game, it introduces key elements like stealth, resource management, and environmental navigation. By the end of this mission, you'll have a better understanding of how to manage your team and approach objectives methodically.

Mission Objective Breakdown

The mission is relatively straightforward, but the challenge lies in your ability to use stealth, minimize combat, and think critically as you work through enemy patrols and obstacles. Here's a breakdown of your objectives for Mission 1:

1. **Infiltrate the Outpost**:
   Your primary task is to enter the enemy outpost without being detected. You'll need to carefully navigate the perimeter and avoid enemy guards while sneaking through openings.
2. **Gather Intel**:
   Once inside, you'll need to locate the enemy documents hidden within the facility. These documents contain valuable intel that will help your team in future missions. Be cautious as the documents are often in well-guarded rooms.

3. **Destroy the Radio**:
   After gathering the intel, your next objective is to sabotage the enemy's communication system by destroying the radio. This will prevent them from calling for reinforcements or raising the alarm about your presence.
4. **Escape to the Extraction Point**:
   Once you have completed your objectives, you'll need to make your way to the extraction point. This area is often near enemy reinforcements, so timing and stealth will be key to making it out unscathed.

Step-by-Step Walkthrough

Phase 1: Infiltrating the Outpost

1. **Assess the Situation**:
   As soon as the mission starts, take a moment to survey the area. You'll see enemy patrols moving along set routes. Use the **pause feature** to plan your movements carefully. This is a great time to position your commandos and get a feel for enemy patrol patterns.
2. **Sneak Past the Guards**:
   The Green Beret is your go-to commando for taking out enemies silently. If there are lone guards in your way, use his melee ability to incapacitate them quietly. Be sure to move their bodies afterward so other enemies don't spot them.
3. **Use the Spy for Disguises**:
   The Spy can disguise himself as an enemy soldier, allowing him to move around freely without alerting guards. Have the Spy infiltrate restricted areas and access locked rooms. Keep an eye on the guards' patrol routes and move when they are out of sight.
4. **Move Stealthily**:
   Always crouch and move slowly using the **Shift** key to reduce the noise your commandos make. Use the environment to your advantage hide behind crates, walls, and other objects to avoid detection. The fewer enemies you engage, the easier it will be to complete the mission without unnecessary combat.

Phase 2: Gathering Intel

1. **Locate the Documents**:
   Once inside the outpost, your goal is to find and collect the intelligence documents. These are typically stored in secured

rooms, so you may need to use the Spy to unlock doors or access restricted areas.

2. **Avoid Detection**:
As you move through the outpost, take note of the guards' patrol patterns. If the documents are in a room with multiple guards, wait for the right moment to slip in unnoticed. You can also use distractions (like throwing a rock) to divert the guards' attention.

3. **Take Extra Care**:
When gathering intel, be sure not to rush. Pay attention to any hidden rooms or areas where enemies may be lurking. Always pause to evaluate the situation before making a move to ensure you're not walking into an ambush.

Phase 3: Destroying the Radio

1. **Locate the Radio**:
After acquiring the intel, your next objective is to destroy the enemy radio. This is typically located in the central command room of the outpost. Use the Spy to sneak past any guards that might be stationed there.

2. **Use Explosives**:
If the mission has allowed you to collect explosives, you can use them to destroy the radio. The Sapper's dynamite is effective for this task, but be mindful of the noise it creates. Alternatively, the Green Beret can plant a charge discreetly if necessary.

3. **Disable the Communication**:
Once you've planted explosives or set up sabotage, ensure you move to a safe distance before detonating the charges. You don't want to alert enemies prematurely. Use the pause function again to coordinate this action and give your team time to retreat.

Phase 4: Extraction

1. **Head to the Extraction Point**:
With the mission's main objectives completed, the final task is to reach the extraction point. This is typically located outside the main facility, where enemy reinforcements may arrive.

2. **Plan Your Escape Route**:
As you move toward the extraction point, you'll encounter additional patrols and possibly alerted enemies. Be sure to use distractions or take enemies out quietly to clear the path. Stay in the shadows and avoid confrontation as much as possible.

3. **Extract and End the Mission**:
    Once you reach the extraction point, the mission will end, but don't get too relaxed. You'll need to ensure all of your commandos make it to the safe zone before completing the mission. If one of your team members gets caught, you may have to abort and restart from the last checkpoint.

Key Tips for Success

- **Use the Pause Feature**: As you move through the outpost, use the **pause** function to plan ahead. This allows you to issue commands to all commandos at once and ensures that you're making the best move possible.
- **Coordinate Distractions**: If you're in a tight spot, use distractions like rocks or other items to lure enemies away from critical areas, allowing your team to move freely.
- **Minimal Combat**: This mission favors stealth over combat. Try to avoid firefights unless absolutely necessary, as they will alert the enemy and make the mission much harder.
- **Quick Saves**: Save your game often, especially after completing key objectives. This will allow you to quickly reload if things go wrong without losing too much progress.

6.2 MISSION 2: INFILTRATING THE ENEMY BASE

In *Commandos: Origins*, Mission 2, *Infiltrating the Enemy Base*, ramps up the complexity and introduces more advanced tactics. You will need to apply everything you learned in the previous mission while facing new challenges such as increased enemy patrols, more heavily fortified locations, and a higher emphasis on teamwork and coordination. This mission pushes your abilities to infiltrate, gather intel, sabotage enemy resources, and escape without detection.

Mission Objective Breakdown

The objectives in Mission 2 are more demanding and will require you to think ahead and use your commandos' unique skills to your advantage. Here's a breakdown of the key objectives:

1. **Infiltrate the Enemy Base**:
   Your first goal is to infiltrate the enemy base, avoiding detection by guards and security systems. The base is filled with enemy patrols and surveillance cameras, so stealth is crucial.
2. **Gather Enemy Intel**:
   Once inside, you need to find and acquire valuable enemy intel hidden within the base. This intel will help you with future missions and give you insight into the enemy's next steps.
3. **Sabotage the Enemy's Communications**:
   After gathering intel, you'll need to disable the enemy's communication systems, ensuring that they cannot alert reinforcements or report your presence.
4. **Extract from the Base**:
   Once your objectives are complete, you'll need to extract your team safely. Enemy patrols will be on high alert, so timing and stealth will be crucial for avoiding detection during your escape.

Step-by-Step Walkthrough

Phase 1: Infiltrating the Enemy Base

1. **Survey the Area**:
   Before moving forward, take the time to survey the enemy base. The terrain around the base will have different points of entry, such as side gates, fences, or hidden openings. Start by observing the guards' patrol routes and the positioning of cameras. The Spy can use his disguise to blend in with the enemy's patrols, which will be useful for getting close to key locations without raising suspicion.
2. **Use Disguises to Blend In**:
   If you're not already familiar with the mechanics, the Spy's disguise is invaluable for this mission. Have him disguise himself as an enemy soldier and sneak past patrols. The Green Beret can follow behind, staying low and using melee takedowns if necessary. If you're not using the Spy, make sure to use the environment for cover and only move when the guards' line of sight is clear.
3. **Avoid Detection by Cameras**:
   The enemy base has surveillance cameras that can trigger alarms if they detect you. Your team must stay out of the cameras' line of sight, moving between areas where the camera doesn't have a clear view. You can also use the environment, such as turning off

the power supply if possible, to disable the cameras temporarily. Alternatively, the Spy can use his abilities to sneak around them while the rest of the team stays hidden.

Phase 2: Gathering Enemy Intel

1. **Locate the Intel**:
   Once inside the base, you will need to locate the room containing the intel. This is usually hidden in a secured office or a high-security area. Use the Spy to unlock doors or bypass security systems. You may also need to use the Green Beret's strength to carry any sensitive items or documents back to the rest of your team without alerting the guards.
2. **Use Stealth and Distraction**:
   If the room is guarded, you will need to wait for the right moment to sneak in. Use distractions such as throwing rocks or cans to lure guards away from the door. Make sure to pickpocket any guards who might have keys to locked rooms or access points, which will make your job easier.
3. **Secure the Intel**:
   Once you've gathered the intel, make sure to store it with a commando who is out of sight from enemy patrols. If you're using the Green Beret to carry the intel, remember that his movement will be slower while carrying items, so position him in a safe location while the rest of the team provides cover.

Phase 3: Sabotaging the Enemy's Communications

1. **Locate the Communications Center**:
   After gathering the intel, your next objective is to sabotage the enemy's communication systems. This can usually be found in the base's central operations room. Use the Spy to infiltrate these high-security areas or take out any guards quietly to create a distraction for the rest of the team.
2. **Plant Explosives or Disable Equipment**:
   Depending on what tools you have at your disposal, you can either plant explosives (if you have the Sapper on your team) or disable communication equipment. The Sapper is essential here, as his ability to plant dynamite or explosives on critical infrastructure can cripple the enemy's ability to call for reinforcements or alert other guards.

3. **Stay Out of Sight**:
   The more noise you make, the higher the chances of getting caught. Take care to disable the communications quietly and quickly. If using explosives, ensure you set a safe distance between your team and the blast site. Timing is critical if you're spotted before detonation, you'll have to deal with increased enemy awareness.

Phase 4: Extraction

1. **Exit the Base**:
   With your objectives completed, it's time to make your exit. The base will be on high alert, and reinforcements may arrive at any moment. Use the Spy to get ahead of the group and scout out the best escape route. Alternatively, have your team move slowly, using cover to stay hidden as they make their way to the extraction point.
2. **Avoid Enemy Patrols**:
   As you move towards the extraction point, enemy patrols will be heightened. Make use of distractions or set traps using the Sapper to delay enemy reinforcements. Keep your team together, making sure to have backup plans in case you're detected.
3. **Use the Pause Feature to Coordinate**:
   If you're moving through a particularly dangerous area, pause the game to issue commands to all your commandos at once. This ensures that your movements are coordinated, and everyone is moving in sync. Using the pause feature strategically will allow you to avoid making rash decisions and getting caught in dangerous situations.
4. **Final Extraction**:
   Once you've reached the extraction point, ensure all of your commandos are safely out of the danger zone before completing the mission. If any of your team members are left behind or spotted during the escape, you'll have to restart from the last checkpoint.

Key Tips for Success

- **Scout Before Moving**: Before moving your team into enemy territory, take time to scout out enemy positions. Use the Sniper's binoculars or the Spy's disguise to gather information and plan the safest route.

- **Stay Patient and Calm**: Stealth missions require patience. Don't rush through areas, and always wait for the right moment to make your move. If you fail, reassess your approach and try again with a better plan.
- **Teamwork is Key**: Each commando has unique strengths use them to your advantage. The Green Beret can deal with melee combat, the Sniper handles long-range eliminations, and the Spy can infiltrate and sabotage. By coordinating your team's actions, you'll be able to navigate through the most dangerous situations.
- **Minimize Combat**: Combat should be your last resort. Stealth and sabotage are much more effective in this mission, so avoid unnecessary fights and eliminate threats only when needed.
- **Use the Environment to Your Advantage**: Always be aware of the environment around you. Use cover, shadows, and elevation to stay hidden and avoid detection.

6.3 MISSION 3: SABOTAGE BEHIND ENEMY LINES

Mission 3: Sabotage Behind Enemy Lines is a critical mission in *Commandos: Origins* that requires precision, cunning, and tactical prowess. As the name suggests, this mission revolves around sabotage, but it also pushes you to deal with a higher level of enemy resistance and more complex objectives. You'll need to infiltrate a heavily guarded enemy installation, plant explosives, and cripple their operations without alerting reinforcements. Stealth and coordination between your commandos will be essential for completing this mission successfully.

Mission Objective Breakdown

In this mission, your key objectives are to infiltrate the enemy lines, sabotage critical infrastructure, and escape undetected. Below is a breakdown of the primary objectives:

1. **Infiltrate the Enemy Base**:
   As usual, your first goal is to sneak into the enemy base without being detected. This requires careful planning, stealth, and knowledge of enemy patrols.
2. **Sabotage Key Infrastructure**:
   After infiltrating the base, you need to plant explosives at specific points within the facility, such as supply depots, fuel tanks, or

communication towers. These acts of sabotage will cripple the enemy's ability to respond effectively to your mission.

3. **Destroy the Enemy Equipment**:
   The mission also tasks you with destroying critical equipment, such as weapons or vehicles, that could aid the enemy's response. This requires a strategic approach to ensure you don't alert other enemies while completing this objective.

4. **Escape the Area**:
   Once the sabotage is complete, you'll need to escape before the enemy raises the alarm. Timing is crucial, and you'll need to move quickly but carefully to avoid encountering any enemy patrols or reinforcements.

Step-by-Step Walkthrough

Phase 1: Infiltrating the Enemy Base

1. **Survey the Area**:
   As the mission begins, take the time to carefully observe the enemy installation. Look for patrol routes, guard positions, and potential entry points. Use the Spy's disguise to blend in with the enemy forces and gain access to the base. If you don't have the Spy in your team, use cover and stealth to stay out of sight.

2. **Plan the Entry**:
   There are typically multiple ways to enter the base, such as climbing fences, sneaking through side gates, or infiltrating through buildings. Use the terrain to your advantage by moving from cover to cover. The Green Beret is ideal for breaking into tight spaces, but make sure to clear the area of guards before proceeding.

3. **Neutralize Threats Quietly**:
   If you encounter enemies, use the Green Beret's silent takedown abilities to incapacitate them without alerting others. Carry bodies out of sight to avoid detection. If you're detected, use the Spy to distract enemies by throwing objects or using his disguise to slip past unnoticed.

4. **Avoid Security Systems**:
   The enemy base likely has security systems in place, such as cameras or motion sensors. These can alert the guards to your presence, so it's important to disable them or navigate around them. The Sapper is particularly useful for disabling traps or

cameras, while the Spy can bypass most security systems using his stealth abilities.

Phase 2: Sabotaging Key Infrastructure

1. **Locate the Critical Targets**:
   Once inside the base, head toward the targets you need to sabotage, which are usually marked on your map or hidden within key sections of the base. The primary targets are often fuel tanks, weapons caches, or communication equipment.
2. **Plant Explosives**:
   The Sapper is the best commando for this task, as he can plant explosives with precision. Carefully plant dynamite on the selected targets. Be sure to clear the area of any guards before detonating the charges. Once the explosives are in place, move your team to a safe distance.
3. **Timing the Explosion**:
   Timing is critical when planting explosives. You can either set a timed delay or manually detonate the charges. Make sure to give yourself enough time to escape the area or complete any additional sabotage objectives before the explosion occurs.
4. **Use Distractions**:
   If the area is heavily guarded, consider using distractions to divert attention away from the sabotage site. Throw objects or use the Spy's abilities to create noise and pull enemies away from their posts. This will give you the window you need to complete your sabotage.

Phase 3: Destroying Enemy Equipment

1. **Find the Enemy Equipment**:
   Once you've planted the explosives, your next task is to destroy enemy equipment. This can include tanks, trucks, or communication devices. These will often be located in specific areas of the base, typically near enemy hangars or garages.
2. **Strategic Destruction**:
   The most effective way to destroy enemy equipment is by using explosives or firearms. The Sapper's dynamite is great for larger targets, while the Green Beret can use a shotgun or other firearms to quickly eliminate equipment or vehicles. Be sure to check the area for enemies who might spot you during the attack.

3. **Minimize Risk:**
   Destruction can create noise, and this will likely attract attention. After destroying the equipment, retreat into cover or find a more secure area to wait for the commotion to die down. If you're spotted, quickly regroup and reset your position before proceeding with the next task.

Phase 4: Extraction

1. **Prepare for Reinforcements:**
   As soon as the explosions go off or your team's location is compromised, enemy reinforcements will arrive. Make sure you've planned an escape route ahead of time. Use the Spy to scout the exit route, or have the Green Beret clear a path to the extraction point.
2. **Escape with Stealth:**
   The extraction phase is as critical as the sabotage itself. Ensure that you move stealthily and avoid enemy patrols. If the base is on high alert, use distractions to keep enemies occupied while you make your escape.
3. **Use the Environment to Evade Detection:**
   Use the environment to cover your escape. Move between cover, such as trees, walls, or vehicles, and stay out of sight. Be mindful of any guards that may be closing in on your position. If necessary, take a detour to avoid high-traffic areas.
4. **Reach the Extraction Point:**
   The extraction point is often located far from the sabotage site, so you'll need to plan your route carefully. Ensure all your commandos are accounted for and make it to the extraction point without being spotted. Once all your team members are at the extraction point, the mission will be complete.

Key Tips for Success

- **Use the Spy's Disguise:** The Spy's disguise is a game-changer when infiltrating the base. Use it to pass through enemy checkpoints and avoid detection while performing sabotage or gathering intel.
- **Take Your Time:** Patience is essential in this mission. Rushing through areas or taking risks can lead to unnecessary conflict or detection. Carefully plan each move and wait for the right moments to strike.

- **Coordinate with Your Team**: Effective teamwork is crucial for success. Use the Green Beret for close combat, the Sapper for sabotage, and the Sniper for cover. Coordinate their actions to complete the objectives as efficiently as possible.
- **Utilize Distractions**: Distractions are a key element in avoiding detection. Use them strategically to divert enemy attention away from your objectives, giving your team the opportunity to complete tasks without interference.
- **Manage Explosives Wisely**: Only plant explosives when you're sure the area is secure. Be mindful of the timing and ensure you've completed all objectives before detonating any charges.

6.4 MISSION 4: RESCUE OPERATION

Mission 4: Rescue Operation introduces a new dynamic to your mission objectives, focusing on rescuing hostages and safely extracting them from enemy territory. This mission is about precision, coordination, and ensuring that all your commandos are working together to avoid any mistakes. Unlike other missions, where the goal is primarily sabotage or intel gathering, in *Mission 4*, you'll be tasked with saving lives while navigating hostile territory, which requires careful planning and execution.

Mission Objective Breakdown

In *Mission 4: Rescue Operation*, the objectives are centered around locating and rescuing prisoners held by the enemy, neutralizing threats, and ensuring a safe extraction. Here's a breakdown of the key objectives:

1. **Infiltrate the Enemy Compound**:
   Your first objective is to infiltrate the enemy compound where the prisoners are being held. Stealth is critical to avoid alerting the guards or triggering alarms that would complicate the extraction process.
2. **Locate the Prisoners**:
   Once inside, you'll need to locate the prisoners, who are often housed in different parts of the facility. The area may be heavily guarded, so careful planning is essential to prevent the mission from becoming compromised.
3. **Rescue the Prisoners**:
   After locating the prisoners, you must free them from their cells or holding areas. This might involve unlocking doors, removing

restraints, or dealing with enemy guards who are watching over them.

4. **Escort the Prisoners to Safety**:
    Once the prisoners are freed, you'll need to escort them to the extraction point. This requires additional caution, as the enemy will likely be on high alert, and you'll need to avoid reinforcements or patrols.

5. **Extract the Prisoners and Team**:
    After reaching the extraction point, ensure that all the prisoners are safely evacuated, and all team members are accounted for. The mission will end successfully when the prisoners are safely extracted.

Step-by-Step Walkthrough

Phase 1: Infiltrating the Enemy Compound

1. **Assess the Situation**:
    Upon starting the mission, observe the enemy compound and scout out the guards' patrol routes, the locations of cameras, and any possible entry points. The Spy's disguise is invaluable here for getting past the outer defenses without being detected. If you don't have the Spy, consider entering through less obvious routes such as side gates or rooftops.

2. **Stealth Movement**:
    As always, keep movement slow and steady. Use cover to move between different areas and stay out of sight from patrolling guards. The Green Beret can eliminate lone guards silently if necessary, but avoid unnecessary combat. Stealth is key to ensuring you can rescue the prisoners without alerting the entire base.

3. **Disable Security Systems**:
    The compound will likely have security systems such as cameras or motion sensors. If possible, disable these systems to prevent being detected. The Sapper is useful here for disabling cameras, while the Spy can avoid them altogether by sticking to blind spots.

4. **Create a Diversion if Necessary**:
    If things get tense, you can use distractions, such as throwing rocks or using the Spy's ability to create noise. This will lure guards away from their posts and allow your team to move past undetected.

Phase 2: Locating the Prisoners

1. **Identify the Prisoner's Location**:
   Once inside the compound, your next task is to find where the prisoners are being held. Typically, prisoners are located in secure rooms, often near the center of the base or in a high-security area. Use the pause feature to assess guard patrols in these areas.
2. **Use the Spy for Reconnaissance**:
   The Spy is the best commando for scouting out areas where the prisoners might be held. Send him ahead to investigate rooms and find the most secure entry points to the prisoner's location. He can also unlock doors or bypass enemy patrols if necessary.
3. **Assess Guard Density**:
   As you approach the prison area, take stock of the enemy forces present. You'll likely face more concentrated enemy patrols here, so it's important to time your movements carefully. The Sniper can be used for long-range eliminations if there are threats that need to be neutralized from a distance.

Phase 3: Rescuing the Prisoners

1. **Secure the Prisoner's Location**:
   Once you locate the prisoners, eliminate any guards standing in your way. The Green Beret is ideal for silently taking out enemies in close quarters, while the Sniper can cover you from afar.
2. **Free the Prisoners**:
   Depending on the facility's setup, you may need to unlock a cell door, cut restraints, or free the prisoners from cages. Use the Green Beret or Spy for these tasks, as they are well-equipped for these kinds of actions. Ensure that you clear the area of guards before freeing the prisoners, as they may be in danger if left unprotected.
3. **Give the Prisoners a Weapon (if Possible)**:
   If there's an opportunity to arm the prisoners, do so. They may assist in fending off enemies during the escape, increasing your chances of success. Ensure that you assign them to follow your team and stay in formation as you move toward the extraction point.

Phase 4: Escorting the Prisoners

1. **Protect the Prisoners During the Escape**:
   Once the prisoners are freed, you'll need to escort them to the extraction point. This is where your team's coordination becomes crucial. Use the Green Beret or Marine to clear any enemy patrols or obstacles in the way while the Sniper covers from a distance. Always ensure the prisoners are out of harm's way.
2. **Avoid Detection**:
   As you move through the compound, stay hidden from patrols and avoid making noise. Use cover effectively and make use of the Spy's distractions if you need to divert enemy attention away from your team.
3. **Use the Environment to Your Advantage**:
   The environment offers plenty of opportunities to hide and create diversions. You can use shadows, walls, and obstacles to keep the prisoners safe while moving toward the extraction point. If you need to slow down pursuing enemies, you can set traps or use explosives to block their paths.

Phase 5: Extraction

1. **Reach the Extraction Point**:
   The final phase of the mission is the escape. The extraction point is often located in a distant part of the base or outside its perimeter. Ensure that all the prisoners are safely with your team as you make your way toward it.
2. **Defend Against Reinforcements**:
   As you make your way to the extraction point, enemy reinforcements will likely be called in. Use the Marine or Green Beret to hold off enemies, while the Sniper picks off distant targets. If you encounter a large group of enemies, consider using explosives to create a barrier or provide a safe retreat for your team.
3. **Escape Safely**:
   Once you've reached the extraction point, ensure that all your team members and prisoners are safely on board. The mission will be complete once the prisoners are extracted and your team has successfully evaded further detection.

Key Tips for Success

- **Keep Stealth at the Forefront**: This mission heavily relies on your ability to stay undetected. Use the Spy's disguise, the Green Beret's silent takedowns, and the Sniper's long-range capabilities to clear the path ahead of you and avoid detection.

- **Use Diversions Wisely**: Distractions can buy you the time you need to make critical movements. If the prisoners are in a heavily guarded area, consider using distractions to draw guards away before making your move.
- **Stay Calm During Combat**: While the objective is primarily a rescue, combat situations will arise. Stay calm and coordinate your team to take out enemies efficiently. Avoid engaging in unnecessary firefights, and focus on completing the mission objectives.
- **Monitor Prisoner Safety**: The prisoners are your priority during the escape. Always ensure they're well-protected as you move toward the extraction point. Having an armed prisoner can make a difference in repelling enemy attacks.
- **Plan Your Exit Route**: Always scout your exit route in advance. Plan around possible reinforcements or unexpected threats. Having a clear escape plan will help you avoid a stressful and chaotic extraction.

CHAPTER 7: SECRETS AND COLLECTIBLES

7.1 HIDDEN AREAS AND EASTER EGGS

One of the most engaging aspects of *Commandos: Origins* is the vast world filled with hidden secrets, Easter eggs, and collectible items. These hidden gems not only provide a sense of discovery and reward but also offer valuable upgrades, lore, and sometimes even affect the outcome of certain missions. This chapter will guide you through the secret areas, Easter eggs, and collectible items scattered throughout the game, ensuring that you don't miss out on these important aspects of the game world.

Commandos: Origins is packed with secret locations and Easter eggs that reward players who take the time to explore beyond the main objectives. These hidden areas are often out of sight from the main mission paths, requiring players to think outside the box and pay attention to environmental details. Here's how you can uncover some of the game's best-hidden features.

1. Secret Rooms and Areas

Throughout the game, you'll come across areas that are not immediately visible or accessible from the main mission routes. These hidden rooms and areas often contain valuable items or provide access to alternative paths.

- **Look for Hidden Passages**: In many of the game's environments, you'll notice small, inconspicuous details that hint at hidden entrances. These can include loose bricks, hidden ladders, or vents. To find these, you'll need to be extra observant. In some cases, the Spy or Sapper can access these hidden areas by either breaking through or unlocking doors.
- **Use the Environment**: Often, secret rooms or paths are concealed behind objects like crates, barrels, or foliage. Move items around, interact with environmental objects, or even push objects like carts to uncover hidden passages.
- **Underground Tunnels**: Certain levels feature underground areas, like tunnels or basements, that are essential for bypassing heavily guarded sections or accessing valuable collectibles. These areas are

typically locked behind a puzzle or require special tools (e.g., the Spy's lockpicks) to access.

- **Unlockable Safehouses**: Safehouses are hidden throughout certain levels and provide a safe space to regroup. These areas often contain extra supplies, weapons, and sometimes even additional mission objectives. To find them, you'll need to search every nook and cranny for unlocked doors or clues left by the enemy.

2. Easter Eggs and Hidden Secrets

Easter eggs in *Commandos: Origins* are fun little secrets placed in the game world by the developers. They are often a nod to the game's history, pop culture references, or simply serve as a fun surprise for players. Here are a few examples of how you can find them:

- **Classic References**: Some Easter eggs are hidden as references to classic *Commandos* games or other popular games in the genre. These could be small items, NPCs, or even scenes that mirror iconic moments from previous games.
- **Hidden NPCs**: Occasionally, you'll find NPCs who don't contribute directly to the mission but offer humorous dialogues, tips, or unlockables when spoken to. These characters are often disguised in plain sight, blending in with enemy forces or hidden in remote corners of the map.
- **Environmental Clues**: Some Easter eggs are tied to the environment itself. Look for unusual objects, graffiti, or markings on walls that seem out of place. These can lead to hidden loot, secret rooms, or even unlock bonus missions that delve into backstory elements or alternate scenarios.
- **Pop Culture References**: In true Easter egg fashion, some areas will nod to popular culture, such as references to famous movies, books, or historical events. Finding these can add an extra layer of enjoyment for those familiar with the references.

7.2 COLLECTIBLE ITEMS: WHAT TO LOOK FOR

While secrets and Easter eggs add an element of surprise, collectible items are integral to enhancing your team's abilities, unlocking hidden content, and adding replay value to *Commandos: Origins*. These items are often well-hidden and require a keen eye to uncover. Here's a look at the most important collectible items you should seek out and how to make the most of them.

1. Weapons and Equipment Upgrades

Collecting weapons and equipment is crucial for improving your team's combat effectiveness and versatility. Many of these upgrades can significantly affect your approach to missions, allowing you to tackle challenges in new and creative ways.

- **Weapon Skins**: Some collectible items are weapon skins that change the appearance of your commando's weapons. While these upgrades don't affect functionality, they provide a cool, personalized touch to your arsenal.
- **Special Ammunition**: Certain levels hide special types of ammunition that can make your weapons more effective, such as armor-piercing rounds for snipers or explosive shells for shotguns. These items often require you to complete challenges or explore hidden areas to find them.
- **Equipment Packs**: Look for collectible equipment packs that give you access to extra tools like additional grenades, landmines, or special gadgets. These can be game-changers, particularly in tough missions where extra tools give you the edge.

2. Lore and Intel Documents

Documents are some of the most common collectibles in *Commandos: Origins*. These items provide backstory information, lore about the game world, and even hints for future missions. These documents are often tied to the story and can be found by searching specific areas or completing side objectives.

- **Intel Files**: Intel files can be found scattered across enemy bases or hidden in locked rooms. These documents can give you insight into enemy movements, upcoming mission objectives, and secret areas to explore. Keep an eye out for these files as they often contain valuable information about the enemy's next moves.
- **Historical Notes and Lore**: Many levels contain notes or documents that provide historical context or deeper narrative layers about the world of *Commandos: Origins*. These are hidden throughout the game and may require you to explore thoroughly.

These notes often provide extra details about the characters, factions, and events that have shaped the game world.

- **Blueprints**: Some collectible documents are blueprints for enemy infrastructure or equipment, which you can use to plan sabotage or missions more effectively. Finding these blueprints can also unlock new strategies for dealing with enemy defenses.

3. Special Collectibles and Bonuses

Beyond weapons and documents, there are other rare collectibles that can provide substantial bonuses or unlock new features in the game.

- **Unlockable Characters**: Some missions feature hidden character collectibles. These unlock new characters or outfits for your team, providing a fun and rewarding way to customize your gameplay.
- **Bonus Objectives**: Completing secret objectives during missions can reward you with special items or unlockable content. These objectives are usually hidden and may involve completing tasks like taking out specific high-value targets, rescuing additional prisoners, or surviving without raising alarms.
- **Hidden Lore Artifacts**: In some levels, you'll find items like photographs, medals, or even old equipment that contribute to the game's lore. These artifacts often provide additional backstory or unlock hidden achievements.

4. Achievements and Trophies

While not strictly "collectibles" in the traditional sense, achievements and trophies are an integral part of *Commandos: Origins*. Completing specific objectives or finding rare items throughout the game will reward you with achievements or trophies, which are often tied to unlocking new game features or additional content.

- **Special Achievements**: Some achievements are unlocked by finding hidden secrets, completing bonus missions, or completing the game without failing certain objectives. These often require a thorough exploration of the game and careful planning.
- **Hidden Trophies**: Similar to achievements, hidden trophies are awarded for completing difficult or challenging objectives. They can be tied to specific in-game accomplishments, like finishing a

mission without raising alarms, rescuing all hostages, or achieving a perfect score on a level.

Key Tips for Collecting Items

- **Thorough Exploration**: The best way to find hidden areas and collectible items is by exploring every corner of the game's levels. Don't rush through the missions take the time to look behind crates, move obstacles, and search for hidden doors or passageways.
- **Use Your Team's Abilities**: Each commando has unique skills that can help you uncover collectibles. The Spy can unlock doors, the Green Beret can move objects, and the Sapper can disable security systems. Make sure to use your team's strengths to access hard-to-reach places.
- **Look for Clues in the Environment**: Many hidden collectibles are indicated by subtle environmental clues, such as unusual markings, crates, or piles of rubble. Keep your eyes peeled for anything that seems out of place or different from the standard environment.
- **Don't Miss Side Objectives**: Some collectibles are tied to optional side objectives. Completing these objectives will often reward you with hidden items, so be sure to check mission maps for any additional tasks.

7.3 UNLOCKABLES AND SECRET MISSIONS

In *Commandos: Origins*, the developers have hidden a variety of unlockable content and secret missions, designed to reward players for thorough exploration, completing specific challenges, and uncovering hidden aspects of the game. These unlockables not only enhance your experience by providing new objectives and stories but also offer a deeper level of engagement with the game world. In this section, we'll explore some of the most exciting unlockables and secret missions you can access during your playthrough.

1. Unlockable Characters and Abilities

Some of the most rewarding unlockables in *Commandos: Origins* are additional characters and abilities that you can access by completing specific tasks or hidden challenges.

- **New Playable Characters**:
  Throughout your journey, you may encounter special characters that can be unlocked after completing certain in-game objectives, such as rescuing specific NPCs, completing bonus missions, or finding hidden areas. These characters usually come with unique abilities that can alter how you approach missions, offering more tactical flexibility. For instance, unlocking a veteran commando with enhanced skills could make tough missions easier.
- **Character Skins and Customization**:
  Some secret unlockables include unique skins or outfits for your existing characters. These skins do not affect gameplay but provide a fun way to personalize your team. Collecting skins may require you to finish side objectives or complete particularly challenging missions.
- **Special Abilities**:
  Unlocking additional abilities for your commandos is a great way to customize your squad to better suit your playstyle. Some abilities might only be accessible after certain milestones, like completing a series of stealth missions without raising alarms or finishing a mission under a specific time limit.

2. Secret Missions

Commandos: Origins includes several secret missions that are not part of the main storyline. These missions are often more difficult than the regular ones, providing a higher challenge for players who seek to test their tactical skills.

- **Unlocking Secret Missions**:
  Secret missions are typically unlocked by completing hidden objectives in the main game. For example, achieving specific achievements or finding hidden items during missions can lead to secret tasks that offer more lore or deeper challenges. These missions may introduce new environments, additional storylines, or specialized objectives that push your skills to the limit.
- **Mission Completion and Rewards**:
  Secret missions often come with significant rewards, such as new equipment, characters, or additional story content. Some might also unlock higher difficulty levels or alternative mission paths. Completing these secret missions not only gives you new gameplay options but also expands the game world and its narrative.

- **Mission Objectives and Mechanics**:
  Secret missions usually involve unconventional objectives that challenge players to think creatively. These could include time-sensitive tasks, stealth-based missions with additional enemies, or scenarios where you need to complete objectives without certain abilities. Completing these objectives will test both your strategic thinking and your ability to adapt to changing circumstances.

3. Unlocking Extra Game Modes

In addition to secret missions, completing certain hidden tasks or challenges can unlock extra game modes. These game modes might provide more complex challenges or change the way you interact with the game.

- **Challenge Mode**:
  Some unlockables include a challenge mode, where you face off against waves of enemies or complete missions with additional restrictions. This mode is designed to push your skills to the limit, and you can earn rewards like new skins or character upgrades for your efforts.
- **Survival Mode**:
  In Survival Mode, your commandos must hold out against waves of enemies as long as possible, testing your ability to manage resources, defend key points, and coordinate your team under pressure.

7.4 HOW TO UNLOCK BONUS CONTENT

Unlocking bonus content in *Commandos: Origins* requires more than simply progressing through the game's main storyline. Often, players must complete additional objectives, find hidden areas, or take on difficult challenges to gain access to these exclusive features. This section will guide you through the best ways to unlock the bonus content that can enhance your game experience and provide exciting new gameplay elements.

1. Completing Hidden Objectives

Many bonus content items in *Commandos: Origins* are unlocked by completing specific hidden objectives during regular missions. These objectives are often not explicitly listed in the mission log and may require you to go off the beaten path.

- **Side Objectives**:
  While the main objectives in each mission are straightforward, there are often additional tasks you can complete, such as rescuing extra prisoners, disabling all security systems, or reaching certain points without being detected. Completing these objectives will unlock additional content, such as special characters, hidden weapons, or new mission areas.
- **Collectibles**:
  Some bonus content can only be unlocked by collecting specific items throughout the game. These might include rare weapons, equipment, or documents that provide extra lore or story content. By thoroughly exploring each mission, you can find these collectibles and unlock hidden bonuses.
- **Challenge Tasks**:
  Certain bonus content is tied to completing difficult challenges. These challenges may involve completing a mission within a time limit, achieving a high stealth rating, or eliminating enemies without using certain tools. Meeting these challenges will unlock game features like secret missions, character upgrades, or special skins.

2. Achievements and Trophies

Achievements and trophies are another key way to unlock bonus content in *Commandos: Origins*. These rewards are often tied to specific in-game feats and offer players a way to earn additional features or rewards by reaching certain milestones.

- **Hidden Achievements**:
  Some achievements are hidden and can only be unlocked by completing very specific tasks. These tasks could involve completing all objectives in a mission without raising alarms, completing a mission with minimal combat, or exploring every hidden area in a map.
- **Trophies for Completion**:
  For players who strive to complete every aspect of the game, certain trophies are awarded for 100% mission completion. Unlocking these trophies may grant special gameplay modes, such as new difficulty settings or new characters.

3. Secret Code Unlocks

In some cases, *Commandos: Origins* includes unlockable content that can only be accessed by entering special codes or completing certain requirements outside of the game. These codes can unlock hidden skins, characters, or game modes.

- **Entering Special Codes**:
  Some unlockables require you to enter special codes in the game's settings or at specific points during gameplay. These codes might be hidden in the game's dialogue or found in external sources like fan forums or official game guides.
- **Accessing Developer Content**:
  Commandos: Origins may include hidden developer content, such as behind-the-scenes images, concept art, or interviews. To unlock this content, you may need to complete certain achievements or find hidden references in the game world.

4. Completing the Game on Higher Difficulties

Once you've completed the game on the standard difficulty, *Commandos: Origins* often allows you to unlock bonus content by playing through the game again on higher difficulty settings.

- **Unlocking Bonus Missions**:
  After completing the game on normal difficulty, playing through it on hard or extreme mode can unlock bonus missions that offer higher stakes, additional challenges, and new content. These missions often reward players with exclusive items or characters that cannot be accessed on lower difficulty settings.
- **New Game Plus**:
  Some bonus content is unlocked by completing the game in "New Game Plus" mode, where you can carry over your progress and unlock additional content as you replay the game with new challenges.

Key Tips for Unlocking Bonus Content

- **Explore Every Nook and Cranny**: Many hidden objectives and collectibles are tucked away in hard-to-find areas. Be thorough in your exploration, as these can unlock some of the best bonus content.

- **Pay Attention to Dialogue and Hints**: Sometimes, the game will drop hints in its dialogue or mission descriptions about secret objectives or hidden items. Make sure to read every piece of information carefully.
- **Replay Missions**: To uncover all the bonus content, consider replaying missions on different difficulty levels or completing additional tasks like collecting all the documents or neutralizing all enemies without being spotted.
- **Take on Side Challenges**: Completing side challenges, such as time trials or stealthy objectives, often unlocks the most rewarding content. Keep an eye out for these extra tasks as you play.

CHAPTER 8: ACHIEVEMENTS AND TROPHIES

8.1 LIST OF ACHIEVEMENTS AND TROPHIES

In *Commandos: Origins*, unlocking achievements and trophies is one of the most rewarding aspects of gameplay. Not only do these serve as markers of your progress and skill, but they also unlock additional content and provide a deeper sense of accomplishment. This chapter will provide you with a comprehensive list of achievements and trophies you can unlock throughout the game, along with helpful tips and strategies for earning them all.

Commandos: Origins offers a variety of achievements and trophies, each of which challenges you to perform specific actions or reach certain milestones. Here is a breakdown of the key achievements and trophies you can unlock as you progress through the game.

Achievement/Trophy Name	Description	Requirement
Stealth Master	Complete any mission without being detected	Complete a mission without raising any alarms or being spotted
Unstoppable Force	Complete a mission without using stealth	Finish a mission while engaging in combat for most of the time
Sharp Shooter	Eliminate 10 enemies with a single shot from the Sniper rifle	Take out 10 enemies with long-range sniper shots in one mission
Perfect Escape	Extract all prisoners without raising alarms	Rescue all prisoners in a mission while remaining undetected

Quick and Deadly	Complete a mission within 30 minutes	Finish any mission in less than 30 minutes
Demolition Expert	Successfully plant explosives in three separate missions	Complete three sabotage missions successfully
All-Out Assault	Eliminate all enemies in a mission	Neutralize every enemy on the map (complete a mission by killing everyone)
Invisible Shadow	Complete a mission without using any weapons	Complete the mission by only using stealth and tactics
Explosives Enthusiast	Use 20 explosive items (grenades, dynamite, etc.)	Use explosives to eliminate enemies or destroy targets 20 times
Master of Disguise	Successfully infiltrate an enemy base using the Spy's disguise	Complete a mission using the Spy's disguise without being caught
All Secrets Revealed	Discover all hidden rooms and Easter eggs	Find every secret room and Easter egg in the game
Victory at All Costs	Complete every mission on the hardest difficulty	Finish the game on the highest difficulty level

Special Achievements

- **Perfectionist**: Complete every mission with 100% efficiency (no failed objectives, all enemies eliminated, no alarms raised).
- **The Lone Wolf**: Complete a mission using only one commando from your squad.

- **No Stone Unturned**: Find every collectible item hidden throughout the game's levels.

These achievements and trophies serve as milestones for your gameplay, encouraging exploration, efficiency, and mastery of different gameplay styles. Some of them are easy to unlock, while others will require skill and patience to earn.

8.2 TIPS FOR EARNING ALL ACHIEVEMENTS

Earning every achievement and trophy in *Commandos: Origins* is no small feat. Some will come naturally as you progress through the game, but others require specific strategies and a deeper understanding of the game mechanics. Below are some helpful tips and strategies for unlocking all of the achievements and trophies.

1. Focus on Stealth for Key Achievements

For many of the achievements, particularly *Stealth Master* and *Invisible Shadow*, stealth will be your best friend. Here are some tips to maximize your stealth gameplay:

- **Use the Pause Feature**: Take advantage of the game's pause function to plan each move carefully. This is particularly helpful when you're trying to sneak past guards or plan takedowns without alerting others.
- **Take Advantage of Shadows and Cover**: Always move between areas of cover, and use shadows to hide your commandos from enemy sight. This is especially useful when moving through well-guarded areas.
- **Time Your Movements**: Enemy patrols move in predictable patterns. Wait for the right moment to move, and be sure to use distractions (like throwing rocks) to lure guards away from critical paths.

2. Maximize Combat for 'Unstoppable Force' and 'All-Out Assault'

If you're aiming for the *Unstoppable Force* or *All-Out Assault* trophies, you'll need to engage in combat. These tips will help you take down enemies efficiently:

- **Use the Right Commando for the Job**: The Green Beret excels in close combat, while the Marine can handle heavy firefights with submachine guns or shotguns. The Sniper should be used for long-range eliminations.
- **Clear Paths Strategically**: If you need to eliminate enemies, focus on removing key threats first. Target enemy snipers, gunners, or any other units that can cause problems for your team.
- **Don't Hesitate to Engage**: If you're going for the *All-Out Assault* achievement, eliminate every enemy you come across. Don't be afraid to take on larger groups of enemies, and use explosives to clear out multiple targets at once.

3. Plan Your Time for 'Quick and Deadly'

Completing missions in under 30 minutes for the *Quick and Deadly* achievement requires careful planning and quick execution:

- **Know Your Objectives**: Focus solely on the mission objectives to save time. Avoid unnecessary exploration or side objectives that can slow you down.
- **Use Shortcuts**: Take the most direct route to your goals. Familiarize yourself with the map and plan your route in advance.
- **Avoid Stealth**: While stealth is important for most missions, time is the key here. Use combat when necessary to speed up the process. Just make sure you're still working towards your goal efficiently.

4. Take Advantage of Explosives for 'Demolition Expert' and 'Explosives Enthusiast'

To earn the *Demolition Expert* and *Explosives Enthusiast* achievements, you'll need to use explosives liberally:

- **Stock Up on Explosives**: Explosives like grenades, dynamite, and mines are your best tools for destroying enemy equipment or clearing paths. Don't be afraid to use them liberally when clearing enemy units or objects.

- **Use Explosives for Distractions**: If you're trying to avoid direct combat but need to progress, use explosives to distract or disorient enemy patrols. This will allow you to move past them without being noticed.
- **Complete Sabotage Missions**: Make sure to complete missions that require sabotage or the destruction of enemy equipment. These missions are perfect for earning both of the explosive-related trophies.

5. Practice Perfect Missions for 'Victory at All Costs' and 'Perfectionist'

For the most challenging achievements, *Victory at All Costs* and *Perfectionist*, every move must be executed flawlessly:

- **Replay Missions for Mastery**: If you fail any objectives or raise alarms, restart the mission and try again. Practice makes perfect, and you'll need to repeat some missions to achieve flawless execution.
- **Work Methodically**: These achievements require precision, so take your time. Focus on eliminating threats without alerting others and completing every objective in the mission.
- **Save Frequently**: Always save your progress frequently, especially when attempting to complete all objectives with high efficiency. This allows you to retry without losing too much progress.

6. Keep an Eye Out for Hidden Items for 'All Secrets Revealed'

To unlock the *All Secrets Revealed* achievement, you'll need to uncover all hidden areas and collectibles throughout the game:

- **Explore Thoroughly**: Don't rush through levels. Take the time to explore every corner and interact with every object to find hidden passages or collectibles.
- **Use Your Commandos' Abilities**: Use the Green Beret's strength to move objects or the Spy's lockpicking skills to open hidden doors. Each commando has a role to play in discovering secrets.

- **Consult the Map**: Sometimes, collectibles or hidden rooms are marked on the mission map. Make sure to check for any areas that seem out of place and need further investigation.

8.3 HIDDEN ACHIEVEMENTS AND HOW TO UNLOCK THEM

Commandos: Origins rewards players not only with obvious achievements but also hidden ones, which are often more challenging and require specific actions or playstyles to unlock. These achievements are designed to test your mastery of the game and often require extra effort, exploration, or strategy to complete. This section will cover the hidden achievements and provide step-by-step instructions on how to unlock them.

1. Hidden Achievement: "Stealth Assassin"

Description:
Complete a mission without alerting any enemies, and without using weapons.

How to Unlock:

- **Play a Stealth-Only Mission**: Choose a mission where stealth is your primary method of completion. The Spy and Green Beret are ideal for this. You must sneak around, avoid all enemy patrols, and complete objectives without raising any alarms.
- **No Combat**: You must rely solely on stealth and tools like distractions to avoid combat. Do not use any firearms, explosives, or other weapons to neutralize enemies.
- **Avoid Detection at All Costs**: Patience is crucial here. Time your movements and wait for enemies to turn their backs or move away from their positions. Use environmental cover and shadows effectively to avoid detection.

2. Hidden Achievement: "Master of Disguise"

Description:
Infiltrate an enemy base by using the Spy's disguise and complete the mission without being caught.

How to Unlock:

- **Disguise as an Enemy**: Use the Spy to infiltrate enemy-controlled areas. He can disguise himself as an enemy soldier, which will allow him to move freely past most guards.
- **Avoid Raising Suspicion**: You must complete the mission without raising any suspicion. This means you cannot be seen acting out of character (e.g., walking too quickly, running, or attacking).
- **Complete All Objectives**: You must successfully complete all mission objectives while maintaining your disguise. Keep an eye on patrol routes and remain in character at all times to avoid being detected.

3. Hidden Achievement: "Perfectionist"

Description:
Complete every objective in a mission with no mistakes, including rescuing all hostages, eliminating all enemies, and not raising alarms.

How to Unlock:

- **Complete the Mission Flawlessly**: This achievement requires you to be meticulous in completing every mission objective. Complete every task whether it's rescuing all hostages or destroying enemy infrastructure without raising any alarms, and eliminate all enemy forces.
- **Plan Every Move**: Use the pause feature to plan ahead and ensure that you execute every task with precision. Avoid any combat unless absolutely necessary and focus on achieving every goal in the mission.
- **Check Your Progress**: Ensure all secondary objectives (such as taking out specific high-value targets or gathering extra intel) are completed. Missing even a small objective will prevent this achievement from unlocking.

4. Hidden Achievement: "Silent But Deadly"

Description:
Complete a mission where you neutralize enemies using only non-lethal methods (melee, distractions, etc.).

How to Unlock:

- **Use Non-Lethal Methods**: For this achievement, you can't kill any enemies. Instead, rely on tools like chloroform, melee takedowns, or environmental hazards to neutralize enemies silently.
- **Avoid Weapons**: Do not use firearms, explosives, or any lethal weapons. Only melee takedowns, environmental traps, and tools that incapacitate enemies are allowed.
- **Complete All Objectives**: Ensure that you complete all primary and secondary objectives while sticking to non-lethal methods. Keep an eye out for additional enemies, and use patience and strategy to neutralize them without violence.

5. Hidden Achievement: "Untouchable"

Description:
Complete a mission without taking any damage.

How to Unlock:

- **Plan Every Move Carefully**: This achievement requires you to avoid all damage. Every time you're spotted or caught in combat, you risk taking damage. Focus on stealth, and make sure your commandos remain out of sight at all times.
- **Avoid Combat**: Combat is a surefire way to take damage, so try to avoid all confrontations. If combat is inevitable, retreat or use distractions to ensure you don't take any hits.
- **Use Team Coordination**: Leverage your team's strengths to avoid getting caught in dangerous situations. Use the Sniper for long-range support and the Green Beret for stealthy takedowns to avoid alerting enemies.

8.4 TROPHY HUNTING FOR COMPLETIONISTS

For completionists, *Commandos: Origins* offers an extra level of challenge with its trophies, which reward players for going above and beyond to fully explore the game's content and achieve all possible milestones. Trophy hunting isn't just about finishing the game it's about uncovering every hidden detail, mastering every challenge, and proving your skills.

1. Focus on Missions and Challenges

To earn every trophy in *Commandos: Origins*, you'll need to focus on completing all missions with full efficiency. Some trophies require specific objectives to be met, such as:

- **No alarms raised**: Complete a mission without alerting the enemy. This often requires a thorough understanding of enemy patrol patterns and optimal usage of your commandos' abilities.
- **All objectives completed**: Complete both primary and secondary objectives in a mission. These can include rescuing extra prisoners, gathering intel, or eliminating every enemy.
- **Time-based challenges**: Some trophies require you to complete missions within specific time limits. These may force you to prioritize speed over stealth, so practice runs may be necessary to achieve the fastest possible completion times.

2. Explore Every Corner of the Game

Some trophies are tied to exploration and discovery. To unlock these, you'll need to thoroughly explore the game world, find hidden collectibles, and complete secret missions. These trophies often reward you with new lore, extra gameplay elements, or even new characters.

- **Finding Hidden Areas**: Some trophies are unlocked by discovering secret rooms, hidden paths, and Easter eggs within the game. Explore every corner of each map, interact with all objects, and be attentive to any environmental clues that suggest a hidden area.
- **Completing All Collectibles**: Certain trophies can only be unlocked by finding all collectible items in the game, such as special documents, weapon upgrades, and secret intel. Completing the collection will grant you access to bonus content and a sense of accomplishment.

3. Achieve Specific Playthrough Goals

There are a number of trophies tied to specific playthrough styles. These trophies will challenge you to complete the game using certain restrictions or approaches.

- **No Kills**: Complete a mission without eliminating any enemies. Use stealth, distractions, and environmental hazards to avoid combat entirely.
- **Solo Playthrough**: Complete a mission with only one commando, such as the Green Beret or Sniper. This will require you to rely on that commando's unique abilities to complete the entire mission.
- **100% Completion**: Complete all missions, find all secrets, and earn every achievement in the game. This trophy will require hours of dedicated play and thorough exploration.

4. Time Your Runs for Speed Trophies

Many completionist trophies are based on completing missions within specific time limits. These trophies reward players who can complete objectives efficiently and with skillful precision.

- **Speedrun the Missions**: Some trophies require you to finish a mission in a set amount of time. These challenges can be tough, as they often involve rushing through the mission while still ensuring success. Use your knowledge of the map, your team's abilities, and your strategic planning to cut down the time needed to complete the objectives.
- **Mastering Each Level**: The best way to earn time-based trophies is by mastering each level and knowing exactly where to go and what to do. After each successful playthrough, tweak your strategy to optimize your time without sacrificing effectiveness.

5. Practice for Perfect Execution

Some trophies require near-perfect execution, such as completing a mission without being detected or without taking damage. These achievements test your skills, patience, and ability to execute perfect stealth runs.

- **No Damage Runs**: Some trophies require you to complete entire missions without taking a single hit. Plan each movement carefully, avoid any unnecessary combat, and use the game's pause function to think ahead before each action.
- **Silent Runs**: Achieving these trophies requires stealth and avoiding detection. Use the Spy for infiltration, the Green Beret for melee takedowns, and the Sniper for covering your movements. Focus on

moving silently and executing quick, non-lethal takedowns when necessary.

CHAPTER 9: ADVANCED TECHNIQUES

9.1 MASTERING HIGH-LEVEL STEALTH OPERATIONS

As you progress through *Commandos: Origins*, the challenges become more complex, demanding a deeper understanding of the game's mechanics and a mastery of advanced tactics. This chapter explores the high-level strategies that will elevate your gameplay. From perfecting stealth to executing advanced combat techniques, these techniques will not only improve your ability to complete missions efficiently but also allow you to approach each level with creativity and precision.

Stealth is a core component of *Commandos: Origins*, and as you advance, you'll need to refine your ability to remain undetected, handle multiple guards, and execute complex maneuvers without raising alarms. High-level stealth operations require more than just hiding in shadows; they require you to think several steps ahead, using all available tools and the environment to your advantage. This section will break down how to become a true stealth master.

1. Understanding Enemy Patrol Patterns

The key to stealth success is understanding and exploiting enemy patrol routes. Each level is filled with enemy guards whose movements follow specific patterns. Here's how to read and exploit them:

- **Observe Before Acting**: Before moving your team, spend a moment observing the guards. Use the pause feature to carefully track patrol patterns. Understanding when and where enemies will move allows you to plan your approach and avoid detection.
- **Learn the 'Safe Zones'**: Every map has certain areas where enemies are less likely to notice you. These areas are often concealed behind obstacles, in shadows, or in rooms with restricted visibility. Your goal is to get your commandos through these zones without ever coming into the line of sight of a guard.
- **Use Timing to Your Advantage**: Timing is critical in high-level stealth. Wait for the guards to turn their backs or move past key

areas before advancing. Every movement should be deliberate and well-timed to avoid detection.

2. Perfecting the Use of Distractions

Distractions are essential for creating openings in the enemy's defenses. Whether it's drawing attention away from a target or leading a guard away from his post, distractions give you the time you need to make a move.

- **Throwing Objects**: Rocks, bottles, and other small objects are perfect for creating distractions. Throw them to draw guards away from their patrols or to lure them into dead ends where you can silently neutralize them.
- **Setting Off Alarms**: In certain situations, it may be beneficial to create a distraction by setting off alarms or triggering loud machinery. This tactic can redirect enemy attention, allowing your team to move in unnoticed from a different route.
- **Using the Spy's Abilities**: The Spy is a master of deception. In high-level stealth operations, you can use his disguise to infiltrate enemy lines without being spotted. This allows you to gather intel, unlock doors, and disable alarms all without triggering suspicion.

3. Managing Multiple Guards

As the difficulty increases, you'll encounter multiple guards who need to be dealt with simultaneously. The key to managing these situations is understanding your surroundings and being patient.

- **Eliminate Guards One by One**: When dealing with multiple enemies, it's important to isolate them. Use distractions to separate guards from each other, then take them down silently, one by one, when they are alone. Be quick, as there is a limited window of opportunity before reinforcements arrive.
- **Environmental Hazards**: Use the environment to your advantage. Push enemies into water or electrical hazards, set up traps, or lead them into explosive areas. The more you can manipulate the environment, the fewer enemies you'll need to deal with directly.
- **Use Commandos' Abilities in Tandem**: The Green Beret, Sniper, and Spy can all complement each other when dealing with multiple enemies. The Sniper can take out enemies from a distance, the Green Beret can eliminate threats up close, and the Spy can sneak

behind enemy lines to disable critical security features or open up paths for the rest of your team.

4. Timing and Patience: The Heart of Stealth

When engaging in high-level stealth operations, the most critical elements are patience and timing. Moving too quickly or rushing your decisions can easily result in detection. Here's how to stay calm and precise under pressure:

- **Wait for the Right Moment**: Never rush through areas with multiple guards. Wait for the perfect moment when enemies are far enough apart to avoid detection. This can mean waiting for several minutes in some situations, but it's necessary for success.
- **Practice Patience**: Learning to be patient is crucial in stealth gameplay. Sometimes, the best action is to do nothing at all. Stay hidden, observe the patterns, and act only when the time is right.

9.2 EFFECTIVE USE OF ADVANCED COMBAT SKILLS

While stealth is often the preferred approach in *Commandos: Origins*, there will be times when you need to engage in combat. Mastering advanced combat skills is essential for overcoming these challenges and ensuring your team's survival. This section will cover the most effective combat techniques and how to utilize them to gain the upper hand in difficult situations.

1. Mastering Weapon Handling

Each commando in *Commandos: Origins* has a unique set of weapons, and mastering their use is crucial to effective combat. Here's how to get the most out of your weapons:

- **Sniper Rifles**: The Sniper is perfect for eliminating high-priority targets from a distance. For maximum effectiveness:
    o **Aim for the Head**: Headshots deal the most damage and can eliminate enemies in one shot.
    o **Use Cover**: Position your Sniper in a high vantage point where they have a clear line of sight. Make sure to use environmental cover to avoid detection.

- **Shotguns and Submachine Guns**: The Marine excels with these close-range, high-damage weapons. Use these when engaging enemies in tight spaces or when you need to clear rooms quickly.
  - **Close-Quarter Combat**: Shotguns are great for taking out multiple enemies in close proximity. Use them when you need to storm an area with multiple guards.
  - **Spray and Pray**: Submachine guns can cover a wide area with rapid-fire shots. Use them in situations where you need to quickly suppress enemy fire or clear a path.

2. Timing and Positioning in Combat

In advanced combat, it's not just about having the right weapons it's about knowing when and where to engage.

- **Use Elevation for an Advantage**: High ground gives you a strategic advantage in combat. From elevated positions, you can avoid incoming fire and take out enemies from a safe distance. The Sniper should always prioritize high ground when possible, while the Green Beret can use it to approach enemies unnoticed.
- **Flanking and Suppression**: Flanking is a powerful combat technique. Have your team approach enemies from multiple angles to trap them in a crossfire. Suppress enemy positions with machine gun fire or grenades, then use the Green Beret or Marine to close in and neutralize the threats.
- **Use Cover Effectively**: Always move from cover to cover. Never stand in open areas where you're an easy target. Use walls, crates, and other environmental elements to shield your team from enemy fire.

3. Advanced Combat Techniques: Grenades and Explosives

Grenades and explosives are invaluable tools in combat, especially when facing large groups of enemies. Here's how to make the most of them:

- **Timed Explosives**: The Sapper is essential for placing explosives, but timed detonations can be used to trap enemies. Plant explosives in enemy rooms or along their patrol routes, then detonate them when they're within range. This will cause maximum damage and chaos.

- **Grenade Tosses**: Throwing grenades can eliminate clusters of enemies in one move. Aim for tight groups of enemies or rooms where multiple guards are stationed together. Be mindful of your position to avoid damaging your own team.
- **Flashbangs**: Use flashbangs to disorient enemies before charging in. This gives you the element of surprise, allowing your team to take advantage of the confusion. Flashbangs are particularly useful in confined spaces or when you need to neutralize multiple enemies quickly.

4. Team Synergy in Combat

While individual combat skills are important, the true strength of your team lies in how well they work together. Synergy is the key to overcoming tough combat scenarios.

- **Sniper and Spotter**: The Sniper works best when paired with a teammate who can spot enemies. The Green Beret or Marine can scout out enemy positions, alert the Sniper, and provide cover while the Sniper takes out targets from a distance.
- **Green Beret and Spy**: The Green Beret excels in close combat, while the Spy is perfect for silently disabling enemies. Use the Spy to infiltrate enemy positions, then have the Green Beret move in to finish off the guards once they're isolated.
- **Marine and Sapper**: Use the Marine as your frontline fighter, with the Sapper in the backline planting explosives or disabling enemy fortifications. This combination ensures that the team remains balanced, with both offensive and defensive capabilities.

9.3 MULTI-CHARACTER COORDINATION FOR COMPLEX MISSIONS

As you progress through *Commandos: Origins*, the complexity of missions increases, requiring more sophisticated coordination between your team members. Mastering the art of multi-character coordination is vital for completing complex missions successfully. Each commando has unique abilities, and knowing how to combine their strengths will allow you to tackle the toughest challenges, from stealthy infiltration to full-scale assaults. In this section, we will explore strategies to maximize the potential of your team through precise coordination.

1. Assigning Roles Based on Mission Needs

The first step in mastering multi-character coordination is understanding the strengths and weaknesses of each commando. Each member of your team brings something unique to the table, and knowing when and how to utilize these abilities can make all the difference.

- **The Green Beret**: As your all-rounder, the Green Beret excels in melee combat, carrying objects, and stealth. He's versatile enough to take on a wide range of tasks, from neutralizing enemies quietly to handling physical tasks like opening doors or moving heavy objects.
- **The Sniper**: The Sniper is ideal for long-range eliminations, and his ability to take out targets from a distance is crucial for providing cover for your team. He works best when positioned in high areas or vantage points, offering support while the rest of the team moves in closer.
- **The Sapper**: The Sapper is essential for sabotage and demolitions. Use him to plant explosives on enemy equipment or fortifications. He can also disarm traps, which will be crucial for getting your team through heavily booby-trapped areas without taking damage.
- **The Spy**: The Spy is a master of infiltration and deception. He can disguise himself as an enemy soldier, unlock doors, and disable alarms. The Spy is most useful in the early phases of a mission, allowing you to get close to enemies without raising suspicion.
- **The Marine**: The Marine is a heavy hitter. His strength lies in direct combat, using powerful firearms to neutralize large groups of enemies. He's ideal for when things get loud and aggressive, offering the muscle to push through tough situations.

2. Using the 'Pause and Plan' Feature

One of the most effective ways to coordinate your team's actions is through the game's pause feature. This allows you to issue commands to all commandos at once, ensuring they move in harmony and execute their actions without hesitation. Here's how to use it effectively:

- **Simultaneous Actions**: When you need to take out multiple enemies or complete a series of tasks, pause the game and issue commands to your entire team. For example, have the Sniper take out a guard from a distance while the Green Beret neutralizes another one up close. Timing their actions perfectly ensures the mission goes smoothly.

- **Escape Plans**: When you're ready to retreat or move to the extraction point, pause the game and plan your escape route. Have each commando take a different path to avoid drawing attention, and assign roles for defensive cover if necessary.
- **Handling Surprises**: If you encounter unexpected situations such as being spotted or a backup alarm going off pause the game immediately to assess the situation. You can then issue commands for damage control, such as setting up a defensive perimeter or switching to a more aggressive tactic.

3. Coordinating Multiple Commandos in Combat

During combat-heavy missions, coordination becomes even more critical. Having each commando act independently is a recipe for failure. Instead, you must think of your team as a well-oiled machine, each part working together seamlessly to eliminate enemies and complete objectives.

- **Using the Sniper as a Spotter**: In larger combat scenarios, the Sniper should act as the team's eyes. Place him in a high vantage point, and use his long-range shots to eliminate high-value targets or suppress enemy fire while the rest of the team moves in closer.

- **Flanking Maneuvers**: To deal with enemies in fortified positions or large groups, use the Green Beret and Marine for direct assaults while the Sniper provides cover. The Spy can be used to infiltrate and disable enemy communications or alarms to create confusion, giving the team more time to eliminate threats.
- **Supporting Each Other**: The Sapper can be used to disable enemy traps or explosives, while the Marine clears a path. The Green Beret can clear rooms, and the Spy can gather intel and open locked doors. Each member's strengths should complement the others to ensure a fluid, tactical approach.

4. The Role of the Spy in Multi-Character Coordination

The Spy is often your team's most important asset in the early stages of a mission, as he can infiltrate enemy positions and gather crucial information.

However, his role doesn't stop there. The Spy is essential in multi-character coordination for several reasons:

- **Distraction and Diversion**: The Spy can create distractions by throwing objects or using his disguise to lure guards away from important areas. This gives your other team members the freedom to move in undetected and accomplish their tasks.
- **Unlocking Pathways**: The Spy can unlock doors or gates that the Green Beret or other team members cannot. By using the Spy to open restricted areas, you can give your team access to hidden rooms or escape routes that would otherwise be unavailable.

9.4 USING THE TERRAIN FOR TACTICAL AMBUSHES

The terrain plays a pivotal role in *Commandos: Origins*, especially when you're planning tactical ambushes. Leveraging the environment can turn the tide of battle, allowing you to eliminate enemies with minimal risk to your team. This section focuses on how to use the terrain strategically for ambushes and tactical advantage.

1. High Ground Advantage

One of the most powerful tactical advantages in *Commandos: Origins* is the ability to take high ground. This can be used both for ambushing enemies and for providing overwatch.

- **Sniper Vantage Points**: The Sniper thrives in high ground situations, where he can pick off enemies from a distance without being detected. Use elevated positions like rooftops, hills, or towers to gain a clear line of sight on enemy patrols.
- **Flanking from Above**: Use elevated terrain to gain an advantage during combat. Have your commandos move around the side or over rooftops to catch enemies off-guard. High ground allows you to avoid direct engagement with large enemy groups, picking them off one by one.
- **Ambush Locations**: When positioning your team for an ambush, high ground allows you to trap enemies in a confined space. For example, if the enemy is moving through a narrow alley, positioning

your team above them gives you the opportunity to strike when they are below, trapped in a kill zone.

2. Natural Barriers for Cover

The environment is full of natural barriers such as trees, rocks, and buildings that can provide cover during your ambush. These barriers are perfect for setting up surprise attacks and limiting the risk of being detected.

- **Luring Enemies into the Open**: Use the terrain to funnel enemies into confined areas where your team can attack with minimal resistance. Place obstacles or set traps to lead enemies into choke points, then ambush them from behind cover.
- **Blocking Retreat Routes**: If you are planning an ambush, use the terrain to block any escape routes. Position obstacles like crates or fallen logs near enemy retreat paths to limit their options and ensure they cannot flee once the battle begins.
- **Environmental Traps**: Some environments offer the possibility to trigger natural hazards, like rocks falling from cliffs or trees that can be used to block or crush enemies. Always keep an eye on your surroundings for opportunities to use the terrain to your advantage.

3. Trapping Enemies with Terrain Features

In *Commandos: Origins*, the use of terrain features is not just about finding cover it's about setting traps and using environmental hazards to take out enemies.

- **Setting Traps in Narrow Passages**: When you know that enemies will be forced to travel through a narrow passage, use explosives or environmental objects to set traps. The Sapper's dynamite can be particularly effective in these situations, taking out large groups of enemies at once.
- **Water Hazards**: Some levels feature bodies of water that can be used to drown enemies or block their path. Use the terrain to force enemies into water and then neutralize them from a safe distance.
- **Using Sound and Distractions**: Terrain can also be used to create noise. Throw objects into specific locations to draw enemies into a vulnerable position. Once they are in the right spot, use your commandos to take them out.

4. Urban Terrain for Urban Warfare

Urban environments in *Commandos: Origins* offer complex terrain that can be used for advanced tactics. Buildings, alleyways, rooftops, and narrow streets are perfect for setting up ambushes and exploiting enemy weaknesses.

- **Rooftop Skirmishes**: Use buildings and rooftops to jump between structures and flank the enemy. This gives you the ability to take out enemies without being noticed by others in the area.
- **Alleyway Ambush**: In city environments, alleyways and narrow streets can act as natural chokepoints. Set up your commandos in these areas to surprise enemies as they enter. Use explosives, melee attacks, or grenades to disrupt their formation and quickly neutralize them.

CHAPTER 10: TROUBLESHOOTING AND COMMON ISSUES

10.1 SOLVING GAMEPLAY GLITCHES AND BUGS

Commandos: Origins offers an exhilarating tactical experience, but like all complex games, players may encounter occasional glitches, bugs, or performance issues. This chapter will guide you through some common problems you may encounter and offer solutions and tips for resolving them. By the end of this chapter, you'll be equipped to troubleshoot issues efficiently, ensuring that you can enjoy the game without interruptions.

No game is entirely free from bugs, and *Commandos: Origins* is no exception. These glitches can range from minor visual issues to more serious gameplay-affecting problems. Fortunately, many of these can be resolved with some simple troubleshooting steps.

1. Character Pathfinding Issues

One of the most common issues players encounter is pathfinding problems, where a character may refuse to move to a designated location or takes a circuitous route.

- **Solution**:
    - **Use the Pause Function**: When you notice pathfinding issues, pause the game to reevaluate the situation. Sometimes, simply resetting the character's path or issuing commands from a different angle can help resolve the issue.
    - **Move Slowly**: If the character is having difficulty navigating complex terrain, try moving them one step at a time. This can sometimes bypass pathfinding errors by reducing the complexity of the movement.
    - **Clear Obstacles**: Ensure that there are no obstacles blocking the character's path. Sometimes, small objects like crates or barrels may cause characters to behave erratically, so clearing the area can help.

2. Inconsistent AI Behavior

At times, enemy AI or even your team members may not behave as expected. For instance, enemies may stand idle instead of patrolling, or your commandos may take too long to respond to commands.

- **Solution**:
    - o **Check for Overloaded Commands**: If your AI team members are unresponsive, it might be due to too many queued commands. Try issuing one command at a time and ensure there's no conflict between them.
    - o **Reposition Units**: Sometimes, repositioning your commandos slightly can help reset their behavior, especially if they're stuck or not executing a move as expected.
    - o **Adjust AI Difficulty**: If the enemy AI seems too passive or erratic, check your game settings. Lowering or increasing the AI difficulty may resolve some erratic behaviors and provide a better challenge.

3. Mission-Blocking Bugs

Certain bugs may prevent you from completing a mission such as an objective not being marked as completed even when you've done everything required or locked doors that should open.

- **Solution**:
    - o **Restart the Mission**: If a mission-blocking bug occurs, try restarting it from the last checkpoint. This can sometimes resolve minor issues that prevent objectives from registering properly.
    - o **Reload Save Files**: If restarting doesn't work, reload a previous save file. Ensure that you're not missing any steps or requirements, as some missions have hidden objectives or timing-based elements that are easy to overlook.
    - o **Check for Patches or Updates**: Sometimes mission-blocking bugs are fixed in patches released by the developers. Check the game's official website or game platform for any available updates that might address these issues.

4. Audio/Visual Glitches

Occasionally, players may experience issues with the game's audio or visual elements, such as missing sound effects, flickering textures, or glitches in cutscenes.

- **Solution**:
  - ○ **Check Audio Drivers**: If the sound is inconsistent, check your audio drivers for updates. Outdated or incompatible drivers can cause audio glitches.
  - ○ **Adjust Visual Settings**: If you're experiencing flickering textures or other visual glitches, try adjusting the game's graphics settings. Lowering the graphical quality or disabling certain effects like anti-aliasing may help resolve these issues.
  - ○ **Verify Game Files**: On PC platforms, you can verify the integrity of the game files through the platform's client (e.g., Steam or Epic Games Store). This will ensure that no files are corrupted and that the game runs smoothly.

10.2 PERFORMANCE OPTIMIZATION TIPS

Commandos: Origins is a graphically demanding game, and players with older hardware or less powerful systems might experience performance issues, such as lag, stuttering, or low frame rates. This section provides tips on how to optimize the game's performance and ensure smooth gameplay.

1. Adjusting Graphics Settings

One of the most effective ways to improve performance is by lowering the game's graphics settings. Here's how to do it:

- **Resolution**: Lowering the game's resolution can significantly improve frame rates, especially if you're playing on a system with limited processing power. Try reducing the resolution by one or two settings (e.g., from 1920x1080 to 1280x720) to see if it makes a difference.
- **Texture Quality**: Reducing texture quality can have a big impact on performance, especially on older systems. Set textures to "Low" or "Medium" instead of "High" for smoother gameplay.
- **Shadow Quality**: Shadows can be demanding on system resources, so lowering shadow quality can help boost performance. Set shadow quality to "Medium" or "Low" to improve frame rates.

- **Anti-Aliasing**: Anti-aliasing is a visual effect that smooths jagged edges but can significantly affect performance. Disabling anti-aliasing or setting it to a lower level (such as 2x or 4x) can improve performance on less powerful systems.

2. Updating Drivers

Outdated drivers can cause performance issues and even crashes in some cases. Ensuring that your hardware drivers are up-to-date can help improve the game's performance and stability.

- **Graphics Card Drivers**: Always update your graphics card drivers to the latest version from the manufacturer's website (NVIDIA, AMD, Intel). New drivers can optimize performance and fix known issues with specific games.
- **Audio Drivers**: Updating your sound drivers can also improve audio performance, preventing stuttering or crackling sounds during gameplay.

3. Closing Background Applications

Running other programs in the background while playing *Commandos: Origins* can consume system resources, leading to decreased performance. To ensure optimal performance:

- **Close Unnecessary Programs**: Before launching the game, close any programs that you don't need, such as web browsers, music players, or productivity tools. These programs can take up valuable CPU, RAM, and disk resources.
- **Disable Background Services**: In some cases, background services (like Windows Update or syncing applications) can slow down your computer. You can disable these temporarily by opening the Task Manager and ending any unnecessary processes.

4. Overclocking Your System (Advanced Users)

For users with higher-end systems or experience with hardware modifications, overclocking your CPU or GPU can improve performance in *Commandos: Origins*. Overclocking increases the clock speed of your components, allowing them to process tasks faster. However, be cautious:

- **Use With Caution**: Overclocking can cause instability or overheating if not done carefully. Always use manufacturer-approved tools and ensure that your system has adequate cooling.
- **Monitor Temperatures**: Use monitoring software to track your CPU and GPU temperatures while gaming. If temperatures rise too high, it could damage your hardware, so make sure your system remains cool during gameplay.

5. Ensuring Sufficient Storage Space

Performance can also be affected if your system's hard drive or SSD is near capacity. Ensuring that you have enough available storage space can help prevent slowdowns, especially when the game needs to access large files.

- **Free Up Space**: Make sure you have at least 10-20% of your hard drive's capacity free. Delete unnecessary files or move data to an external drive if needed.
- **Defragment Your Hard Drive (HDD)**: If you're using a traditional hard drive (HDD) instead of an SSD, defragmenting the drive can help improve loading times and performance. Use the built-in disk defragmenter on your operating system for this task.

6. Enabling V-Sync and Frame Rate Limiting

V-Sync can help prevent screen tearing and improve visual smoothness by syncing your frame rate with your monitor's refresh rate. Similarly, limiting your frame rate can improve performance by reducing unnecessary strain on your system.

- **Enable V-Sync**: If you experience screen tearing, try enabling V-Sync in the graphics settings to sync the frame rate to your monitor's refresh rate. This will smooth out the image and reduce visual artifacts.
- **Limit Frame Rate**: If your system is struggling with performance, consider limiting your frame rate to a lower value (e.g., 30 or 60 FPS). This can prevent your system from working too hard to render unnecessary frames, leading to smoother gameplay.

10.3 FREQUENTLY ASKED QUESTIONS (FAQ)

This section addresses the most common questions players have while playing *Commandos: Origins*. Whether you're encountering technical issues, looking for gameplay tips, or seeking clarification on game mechanics, these answers should help resolve any confusion you might have.

1. How do I improve my team's coordination?

To improve coordination, make sure you're fully utilizing the game's pause and plan feature. This allows you to issue commands to all your commandos at once, ensuring they act in unison. Focus on each character's strengths use the Spy for infiltration, the Sniper for long-range support, the Green Beret for close combat, and the Sapper for demolitions. The key is timing and strategic positioning to create synergy between your team.

2. What do I do if the game crashes during a mission?

If the game crashes, try the following steps:

- **Update your system drivers** (especially graphics and audio drivers).
- **Verify the integrity of the game files** if playing on a platform like Steam.
- **Lower the graphical settings** to reduce the load on your system.
- **Check for software conflicts** by closing background programs or disabling unnecessary services.

If the issue persists, try restarting the mission from the last checkpoint or reloading a previous save file.

3. Why are my character commands not responding?

If your command inputs aren't being recognized, the issue might be with your keyboard or controller setup. Try the following:

- **Restart the game** to reset input configurations.
- **Check the key bindings** in the game settings to ensure they are properly mapped.
- **Disconnect and reconnect any controllers** if you are using one.
- **Ensure your hardware drivers** (keyboard, mouse, or controller) are up-to-date.

If none of these resolve the issue, consider resetting the key bindings to default.

4. How can I unlock all the bonus content in the game?

To unlock bonus content, you need to focus on completing hidden objectives and missions. This includes:

- **Completing every mission with different objectives** such as not being detected or finishing within a time limit.
- **Finding all collectibles and hidden areas** in each level.
- **Earning special achievements** by completing unique challenges.

Check the in-game achievements menu for a list of requirements and make sure to explore thoroughly.

5. I'm stuck on a mission. How can I progress?

If you find yourself stuck, try the following:

- **Review your objectives** to ensure you haven't missed something important.
- **Use the pause feature** to carefully plan out your next move. It can help you avoid dangerous situations and optimize your strategy.
- **Experiment with different characters and their abilities**, as certain missions may require you to use the unique skills of a specific commando.
- **Check online guides or forums** for tips on how to complete challenging sections. Sometimes, others may have encountered similar obstacles and can provide insights.

6. Are there any ways to speed up the game's performance?

To improve performance, you can:

- **Lower the graphical settings** (e.g., resolution, shadow quality, texture resolution).
- **Close any background applications** that may be consuming system resources.

- **Ensure your drivers** (especially your GPU and sound drivers) are up-to-date.
- **Check your hardware specs** against the game's recommended settings and make sure your system meets or exceeds them.

7. How can I access hidden areas or Easter eggs?

Hidden areas and Easter eggs are scattered across the game's levels. To find them:

- **Thoroughly explore each mission**. Search behind crates, inside buildings, or behind walls for secret doors or passageways.
- **Use distractions and the Spy's abilities** to access areas that might otherwise be locked.
- **Look for subtle environmental clues**, like unusual markings or items, that indicate something is hidden nearby.

8. Can I customize my commandos or their abilities?

Customization is limited in terms of appearance, but you can adjust your commandos' abilities by focusing on upgrading their skills through achievements and completing side objectives. While you cannot directly change their equipment in-game, unlocking new weapons, skins, and abilities will enhance your team's overall strength.

10.4 HOW TO REPORT BUGS

If you encounter a bug or technical issue while playing *Commandos: Origins*, reporting it to the development team ensures that the issue can be investigated and resolved. Below is a step-by-step guide on how to report bugs efficiently.

1. Check for Known Issues

Before submitting a bug report, check the official game forums, patch notes, or the FAQ section to see if the issue has already been acknowledged. Sometimes, developers may release hotfixes or workarounds for known problems. If you find your issue listed, follow any suggested solutions.

2. Gather Information About the Bug

To help the development team identify and fix the issue quickly, provide as much information as possible:

- **Describe the issue clearly**: Provide a detailed explanation of the problem. For example, if the game crashes, note when it occurs (during a specific mission, after a certain action, etc.).
- **Include system specs**: Provide information about your computer or console, including operating system, processor, graphics card, RAM, and any other relevant details. This helps the team identify potential system-specific issues.
- **Take screenshots or videos**: If the bug is visual or related to gameplay, try to capture the issue with screenshots or video clips. This provides context for the team and helps them recreate the problem more easily.
- **List steps to reproduce the bug**: If possible, outline the exact steps you took before the bug occurred. For example, "I reached the mission checkpoint and then attempted to enter the building, at which point the game froze."

3. Submit Your Bug Report

Once you've gathered all the necessary information, submit your bug report to the official channels:

- **In-Game Reporting**: Many games, including *Commandos: Origins*, have an in-game bug reporting tool. Use this to submit the details of your issue directly to the developers.
- **Official Forums or Support Websites**: If there's no in-game reporting tool, visit the game's official website or forums. Most game developers have a support page where players can submit issues. Look for a "Bug Report" section or contact support form.
- **Email**: If no reporting tools are available, you can email the support team. Include all the relevant details (steps to reproduce the bug, system specs, screenshots/videos, etc.) to help the team resolve the issue as quickly as possible.

4. Follow Up

After submitting your report, you may not receive an immediate response, but developers typically investigate all reported issues. If the bug continues to affect your gameplay, check for updates or replies from the support team. Sometimes, developers will provide patches or workarounds in future updates.

5. Use the Community for Help

While waiting for a fix, the game's community can often provide temporary solutions or advice. Forums and social media groups dedicated to *Commandos: Origins* are excellent resources for finding others who may have encountered the same bug. You might also find unofficial fixes or workarounds shared by fellow players.

CONCLUSION

11.1 FINAL THOUGHTS ON *Commandos: Origins*

Commandos: Origins offers a rich, immersive experience that rewards careful planning, tactical thinking, and the mastery of various gameplay mechanics. Whether you're infiltrating enemy bases, engaging in intense firefights, or executing stealthy sabotage missions, the game presents a variety of challenges that keep players engaged from start to finish. In this final section, we'll reflect on the key takeaways from the game, offering some final thoughts and additional tips to help you succeed in the long run.

Commandos: Origins is more than just a game; it's a test of strategy, patience, and creativity. As you progress through the missions, you'll quickly learn that brute force is rarely the answer. Success lies in your ability to adapt to each scenario, making full use of your team's strengths and the environment around you.

The game's unique blend of stealth, tactical combat, and puzzle-solving ensures that it never becomes monotonous. Each mission presents fresh challenges, from navigating complex enemy defenses to managing limited resources. The diversity of the commandos' skills encourages experimentation with different strategies, offering a new experience with every playthrough.

However, the game does have its challenges. With its demanding mechanics and complex mission structures, *Commandos: Origins* can feel overwhelming at times, particularly for new players. But this difficulty is part of what makes the game so rewarding. Every victory feels earned, and every mission completed is a testament to your growing expertise as a tactician.

As you immerse yourself in the game, keep in mind that it rewards both thoughtful planning and swift execution. Sometimes, the best way to succeed is to be patient, taking your time to learn the patterns, scout the environment, and plan your approach carefully. And when things don't go according to plan, don't hesitate to restart, regroup, and refine your strategy.

Key Takeaways

- **Stealth is Key**: Most missions can be completed more efficiently using stealth, with combat being a last resort. Mastering stealth is crucial to success.
- **Coordination and Strategy**: Using your team's unique abilities in sync with each other is essential. Effective planning and multi-character coordination can make all the difference.
- **Exploration Pays Off**: Take time to explore the environment, as hidden areas, collectibles, and secret missions provide both rewards and deeper insights into the game world.
- **Patience and Precision**: Success in *Commandos: Origins* is rarely about rushing through a mission. Patience, planning, and precise execution are what will help you overcome even the toughest challenges.

In conclusion, *Commandos: Origins* is an excellent addition to the tactical strategy genre. It rewards thoughtful, creative play, and its depth of strategy and complex mechanics offer hours of engaging content for dedicated players.

11.2 ADDITIONAL TIPS FOR LONG-TERM SUCCESS

While *Commandos: Origins* is packed with content, achieving long-term success requires more than just completing the game's missions. To maintain your edge, here are some additional tips that will ensure your success in the long run:

1. Mastering Every Commando's Abilities

Each commando has a unique set of skills, and knowing how to best utilize these skills is essential to long-term success. Spend time mastering each character's abilities and practice using them in different scenarios. For instance:

- **The Green Beret** is perfect for taking out enemies quietly with melee attacks and handling physical tasks like carrying heavy objects. Learning when to use him versus the other commandos can make or break a mission.

- **The Sniper** thrives in long-range eliminations. Practice taking out enemies from a distance while using the terrain to remain hidden.
- **The Sapper** is invaluable for sabotage and clearing explosive obstacles. Use him wisely to dismantle enemy equipment and structures, but don't rush into explosive situations without proper planning.

2. Experiment with Different Tactics

Don't be afraid to try different strategies. The game encourages experimentation, and you may find that one mission can be tackled in multiple ways. Try completing objectives using stealth, then replay the same mission with a more aggressive combat-focused approach. This will give you a deeper understanding of each mission's dynamics and help refine your overall tactical abilities.

3. Take Advantage of the Pause Feature

In high-pressure situations, the ability to pause the game and issue commands is invaluable. Use this feature not only to plan but also to review the battlefield and adjust your strategy as needed. It's an essential tool for ensuring that you don't make rash decisions that could cost you the mission. In addition, it's the best way to manage multi-character coordination, as it gives you the time to issue commands to all your team members simultaneously.

4. Focus on Mission Objectives

While side objectives and collectibles are important for unlocking extra content, focusing on the main mission objectives is the best way to ensure your success. Completing each level efficiently will make you more adept at handling the game's challenges and will allow you to build up the necessary experience to tackle harder missions.

5. Stay Updated on Patches and New Content

Commandos: Origins may receive updates, patches, or DLCs that can introduce new features, bug fixes, or additional missions. Staying updated on these developments will ensure you get the most out of the game and help you address any new issues that may arise. Keep an eye on official channels like the developer's website, forums, or social media for any new content that enhances your experience.

6. Join the Community

Commandos: Origins has a dedicated player community where you can share strategies, tips, and insights with fellow gamers. Participating in these forums or social media groups can provide valuable perspectives on how to approach different missions, as well as help you discover hidden secrets that you may have missed. Engaging with the community will also keep the game fresh as you share your successes and challenges with others.

11.3 KEEPING YOUR SKILLS SHARP: ADVANCED PLAYER RESOURCES

As you progress in *Commandos: Origins*, you'll encounter increasingly complex missions and challenges that demand a high level of skill and strategic thinking. To maintain and improve your gameplay, it's essential to tap into advanced resources and continuously refine your skills. Whether you're looking to improve your tactics, discover hidden game mechanics, or engage with expert players, the following resources will help you sharpen your abilities and stay ahead of the curve.

1. In-Depth Game Guides and Tutorials

The first step toward mastering advanced tactics is to delve into comprehensive guides and tutorials. These resources break down complex game mechanics, provide step-by-step strategies, and offer tips for overcoming difficult missions.

- **Official Game Guides**: The developer often releases official guides that detail every aspect of the game, from basic mechanics to advanced strategies. These guides are an excellent resource for understanding the finer points of *Commandos: Origins*.
- **Expert-Led Tutorials**: Many seasoned players and streamers create detailed walkthroughs and tutorials on platforms like YouTube and gaming forums. These can provide insightful strategies, including unconventional approaches and hidden tips you might not have discovered yet.

- **Strategy Websites**: Websites dedicated to tactical games often feature in-depth guides, mission-specific strategies, and optimization tips. Sites like GameFAQs, IGN, or specialized gaming forums may have expert-written guides that dive deep into advanced strategies.

2. Mastering Advanced Stealth and Combat Techniques

To truly excel in *Commandos: Origins*, you need to push beyond the basics and refine your mastery of stealth and combat mechanics. The following resources are crucial for advancing your skills in these areas:

- **Stealth Practice**: Stealth missions can be challenging, especially when facing multiple enemies. To improve, practice missions where stealth is paramount. Experiment with different character combinations to discover the most efficient tactics for each level.
- **Combat Drills**: Combat scenarios require precision and quick reflexes. Use training modes, if available, to practice combat mechanics, such as weapon switching, melee attacks, and managing multiple enemy types. Developing quick decision-making skills during combat will give you an edge when things get intense.
- **Tactical Gameplay Videos**: Watching skilled players navigate difficult scenarios can provide valuable insights into advanced techniques. Look for "no-damage" or "speedrun" videos, as these players will use advanced stealth, resource management, and combat skills to beat levels under pressure.

3. Analyzing Advanced Mission Strategies

For missions with multiple objectives, complex enemy AI, and various environmental factors, it's important to analyze your approach critically.

- **Replaying Missions for Efficiency**: After completing a mission, go back and replay it to refine your strategy. Focus on improving your time, stealth efficiency, and execution. As you replay, try to find shortcuts or alternative tactics that might be more effective.
- **Speedruns and Challenge Playthroughs**: Engage in challenge playthroughs or speedruns to hone your skills under pressure. This helps improve your ability to adapt to unexpected challenges while maintaining a high level of performance.

4. Keep Up with Game Updates

Commandos: Origins may receive updates, patches, and downloadable content (DLC) that can introduce new mechanics, characters, or features. Staying current with these updates is essential for mastering new strategies and adapting to any changes in gameplay.

- **Patch Notes and Developer Updates**: Always check the patch notes for updates on bug fixes, balance changes, or new game mechanics. Understanding how the game evolves will keep your tactics relevant and allow you to take advantage of any newly introduced features.
- **DLC and Expansions**: New downloadable content often includes additional missions, characters, or abilities that can refresh your playthrough and introduce new tactical challenges. Keep an eye on DLC releases for expanded gameplay options.

11.4 COMMUNITY AND ONGOING SUPPORT

The *Commandos: Origins* community plays a significant role in enhancing your experience, providing ongoing support, and keeping the game alive long after you've mastered its challenges. Engaging with the community and utilizing the support systems can help you tackle tough missions, discover new strategies, and stay up-to-date with the game's developments.

1. Join Online Forums and Discussion Boards

The *Commandos* community is filled with experienced players who share tips, strategies, and solutions to common problems. Participating in these discussions can help you:

- **Exchange Strategies**: Forum threads dedicated to specific missions or character strategies often provide new insights that you might not have thought of. Sharing your own experiences can also help others.
- **Troubleshoot Issues**: If you encounter a particularly difficult bug or technical problem, the community is a great resource for finding solutions. Many players have experienced similar issues and can suggest workarounds or fixes.

- **Discover Hidden Content**: Forums often share secrets, Easter eggs, and hidden game mechanics that you might have missed. This keeps your experience fresh and helps you uncover everything the game has to offer.

2. Engage with Social Media and Streamers

Social media platforms like Twitter, Reddit, and Discord provide real-time updates and community interaction. Following official game accounts and community pages ensures that you stay informed about the latest news, events, and announcements.

- **Reddit**: Subreddits dedicated to *Commandos: Origins* can be an excellent source of detailed discussions, fan theories, and gameplay advice. It's a space where players from all skill levels can ask questions and get answers from the community.
- **Twitch and YouTube**: Watching professional streamers and content creators can introduce you to unique strategies and tactics. Streamers often share their gameplay, providing insight into how they approach challenges and manage difficult missions.

3. Support Channels for Technical Assistance

For any technical issues, glitches, or bugs that you can't resolve through typical troubleshooting, the official *Commandos: Origins* support team is always available to assist.

- **Official Support Website**: Many developers offer dedicated support pages where you can submit bug reports or get help with game-related problems. Always check the FAQ section first to see if your issue has already been addressed.
- **Customer Service**: If you encounter serious technical issues (such as crashes or performance problems that aren't resolved by troubleshooting), contact customer service directly for a more personalized resolution. Be sure to provide them with as much detail as possible, including system specs, steps to reproduce the issue, and any relevant screenshots or videos.

4. Participate in Community Events and Tournaments

Some games host online events, tournaments, or challenges to keep players engaged and connected. *Commandos: Origins* may feature periodic events that offer rewards or new content, providing a chance to compete against others or showcase your tactical prowess.

- **Competitions**: Keep an eye out for any official or community-run competitions. These events often offer exclusive in-game items, leaderboard recognition, or even real-world prizes.
- **Live Streams and Community Events**: Participate in live-streamed events where developers engage with the community, offer tips, or discuss new features. These sessions are a great way to learn from the experts and get firsthand information about game updates.

5. Modding and Custom Content

For players who want to extend the game's life and customize their experience, modding can be a great option. Many games in the *Commandos* series support modding, allowing players to create custom missions, characters, and gameplay modes. Modding can breathe new life into the game, providing endless replayability.

- **Modding Communities**: Join modding communities to discover new content or even create your own. Whether you're interested in new missions, different gameplay modes, or visual enhancements, modding opens up endless possibilities.
- **Modding Tools**: Check for any official modding tools or documentation provided by the developers. These tools will help you design your own content, from new levels to custom assets, and share them with the community.